MY BURNING TONGUE

MEXICAN SPANISH

LEE JAMISON

insiderspanish.com

To my one and only mother-in-law,
Guadalupe Casillas, for giving me
my one and only.

Let the Burning Begin

A CHUBBY-CHEEKED Mexican was chomping on his lunch right in front of me in the company cafeteria. In one hand he clutched a raw hot pepper. With the other he had fashioned a tortilla into a makeshift spoon with which he shoveled the plate's contents into his mouth. After each tortilla load, his other hand telescoped in for another mouth-burning bite. Tortilla. Hot pepper. Tortilla. Hot pepper. It was like clockwork.

"What kind of pepper are you eating?" I asked.

"**Chile de amor**," he smirked.

"**Chile de amor**?" I thought to myself. "What is that?" I had heard of my share of chilies—from jalapeños to chipotles to serranos. But **chile de amor**? *Love* chili? Was that some kind of aphrodisiac?

Sensing my bewilderment, he explained: "Es chile de **a mor**didas." Ah, clever play on words! Literal meaning? Chili one bite at a time.

That made one thing clear: Mexicans love mouth burning. For some, the hotter the pepper, the better the meal. But why? And what does all of this have to do with Mexican Spanish? Why is it that Mexican Spanish is the tongue that burned my mouth?

WHY YOU SHOULD READ THIS BOOK

Capsaicin is the chemical that puts the heat in hot peppers. Similarly, the native words, idioms and sayings that make Mexican Spanish *Mexican* are its linguistic equivalent. They are what give the spice, color and warmth to any language. Just consider for a minute the many benefits of hot peppers and the language parallels. Among other things, they:

- **Stimulate circulation**. In the *New York Times* article *Eating Spicy Food: What are the Effects?* Jane E. Brody writes: "In general, hot, spicy foods are stimulants. They stimulate the circulation and raise body temperature." When you learn to master Mexican Spanish with all the nuances of local speakers, you will stimulate conversations that will circulate much longer. Mexicans will be curious: How did this foreigner learn to speak like us? Questions and more lengthy dialogues will ensue.

- **Make you sweat, causing you to feel refreshed**. As mentioned above, hot peppers raise our body temperature and provoke perspiration. In a hot climate like Mexico's, that's good news. Our bodies feel cooler and invigorated. Let's be honest. Learning to speak like the natives requires work; you will have to sweat for it. But that effort will be rewarded in spades, as your Spanish will be refreshing—even delightful—both to you and the locals.

- **Stimulate the appetite**. The same *Times* article continues: "Peppery foods are also believed to stimulate the appetite by setting off the flow of saliva and gastric juices, a nutritionally important effect for people in tropical areas where the oppressive heat acts as an appetite suppressant." As you get the hang of the local lingo, your appetite for learning more will only increase. This book is not an end, but rather a beginning; it merely whets your appetite for a lifetime of language learning. Don't be put off by the oppressive heat of beginner's adversity. The good results you'll get by applying the suggestions here will prod you on to success.

- **Add color**. Beyond their physiological effects on us, hot peppers add color to a meal. Doesn't presentation also pique your interest and open your appetite to a greater extent? The words, phrases and sayings you will learn here will likewise add greater color to your speech. They will close the sale, get you the job, and help make new friends.

- **Strengthen the immune system**. How is that possible? That's because hot peppers are loaded with Vitamin C. Ounce for ounce they have two and half times more Vitamin C than oranges, thus providing a powerful boost to your immune system. In a similar vein, understanding the subtleties of Mexican Spanish will undoubtedly protect you whether you're at the market or in a dark alley. It could help you discern the difference between a deal and a scam.

- **Add flavor without compromising health**. Do you have high blood pressure? Then your doctor has probably advised you against consuming salt. That doesn't condemn you to a bland diet if you allow hot peppers to come to the rescue. They'll add flavor to your meals without pressuring your arteries. In comparison: How do you feel when you don't understand what you are being told? Or if you can't find the words to express yourself? Your frustration could send your blood pressure spiking. Once again, understanding the locals well and being able to express yourself freely will add flavor to your life and help calm frayed nerves.

- **Create greater alertness**. Finally, the *Times* resumed hot peppers' benefits: "Anecdotally at least, they act as an overall stimulant, producing a titillating, awakening effect and increasing the acuity of the senses." Likewise, your command of the local Spanish will make you alert to opportunities and to dangers.

MEXICAN SPANISH IS A FLAMING JUGGERNAUT

In 2020 the **Instituto Cervantes**, a non-profit agency set up by the government of Spain to promote Spanish language study worldwide, calculated the total amount of native Spanish speakers on the planet at 585 million. Of these, how many speak Mexican Spanish? Let's do some calculations based on the Institute's findings.

First of all, these scholars counted close to 128 million Spanish speakers in Mexico itself, which includes four million "of limited competency"—a reference to second and third generation bilingual Spanish speakers. The key to unlocking the final amount of Mexican Spanish speakers lies in the United States, where they have immigrated en masse for decades. The Institute calculated native Spanish speakers in the US at 41 million. Another 14.9 million are "of limited competency." And let's not forget the 7.7 million illegal immigrants. By adding these figures, we get a grand total of 64 million Spanish speakers in the United States. That makes the USA the second-largest "Spanish-speaking" country in the world!

But that still leaves us with the question: Of those 64 million Spanish speakers in the US, how many are Mexican? Let's turn now to the findings of The Pew Research Center. In a 2017 report they determined that 62% of all Hispanics in the United States were of Mexican origin. If we assume that this percentage has remained steady today, we can extrapolate some 39.7 million Mexican Spanish speakers in the US (64,060,427 × 62% = 39,717,465).

That leads us to add the 128 million total speakers in Mexico to their 39.7 million cousins in the US for a grand total of 167.5 million Mexican Spanish speakers—truly a juggernaut! **Roughly one out of every three Spanish speakers on the planet speaks Mexican Spanish.**

Quite frankly, no other country even comes close. Colombia, with some 50.3 million Colombian Spanish speakers at home (according to Cervantes), and another 1.2 million in the US (according to Pew Research), comes in second place with 51 million speakers. That is less than a third of the Mexican contingent.

By sheer demographics, Mexican Spanish is the hottest variant on the planet. This has only been accentuated by the Mexican film industry. Television shows such as *El Chavo del Ocho, Chespirito* as well as the antics of Cantinflas, Tin Tan, and other comics have introduced new vocabulary not only in Mexico, but the world over. Steamy Mexican soap operas streamed across the globe have popularized some local speech globally. These days Spaniards, Colombians and Puerto Ricans joke of having a **chiripiorca** (See term #399).

It stands to reason that if you had to choose one particular variant in which to hone your Spanish, you would look no further than the variety from the Land of the Aztecs.

WHO SHOULD READ THIS BOOK

Let's first start off by discussing who *should not* read this book. If you are looking for a stale phrase book to discover how to say, "Where is the bathroom?," this volume is definitely not for you. There are already hundreds of other books out there that dispense that basic babble.

Rather, the main target here are medium to advanced Spanish speakers. This volume will help you to personalize your vocabulary and tailor it to the Mexican dialect.

Another considerable group are Mexican-Americans, or as some prefer to be called, **chicanos** (See term #317). You will definitely enjoy the selection found here, as it will reconnect you to your roots and aid you in understanding your relatives, who may still reside in Mexico. Your children, who likely favor English, will find it a valuable resource in understanding spoken Mexican Spanish—especially since everything is explained in plain English. If words were pictures, consider this your family album.

Lastly, Spanish speakers not from Mexico and who are bilingual in English will likewise benefit as you discover what your Mexican neighbors are *really* saying.

IS THIS ANOTHER BOOK ABOUT SLANG?

Although some slang terms are here included, this is not a slang dictionary. Rather, it is a practical guide to colloquial Mexican Spanish. In a few words, it's about the stuff conversations are made of. It includes:

- **Spanish words with special meaning in Mexico**. To understand this, consider: When Americans hear the word *queue*, they might first think of the letter before *r*. Brits, however, will instantly conjure up a line; they wait in a *queue*. Similarly, certain terms mean one thing in Latin America, but something quite different in Mexico. (For examples, see #216, **acordeón**; #220, **grande**; and #367, **coraje**.)

- **Terms originating from indigenous languages**. More than 60 indigenous languages are still spoken in Mexico today, and these have introduced new vocabulary into the local Spanish. Nahuatl above all permeates Mexican Spanish. (See #100, **guajolote**; #299, **jitomate**; and #419, **chapopote**.) Mayan, too, wields a significant influence especially in the Yucatán Peninsula. (See term #282, **hacer chuc**; **xux** in the box beneath #376; and **chop calle** in the box below #417.)

- **Terms that were originally brand names**. Ever clean your ears with a Q-tip? Actually, Q-tip is a brand name, but we now use it as a common noun for a cotton swab. Similarly, some Mexican and foreign brand names have been indelibly etched into local Spanish. (See #421, **claxon**; #423, **combi**; and, #494, **diurex**.)

- **Idioms**. An idiom is a combination of words whose meaning differs from the meaning of their individual components. To illustrate, you might tell someone you are feeling *under the weather. Under the* *weather* is an idiom because the meaning of the phrase has nothing to do with being under anything at all and even less with the weather. As a phrase it means *to not feel well, to be sick*. (See #140, **hacer la barba**; #271, **echar toda la carne al asador**; and #410, **darle el avión**.)

- **Eponyms**. Eponyms are words derived from proper names. *Sandwich* came from the Earl of Sandwich. *Boycott* is derived from Captain Charles C. Boycott. And, while we're discussing mouth-burning, how could we forget *Fahrenheit*? Gabriel Daniel Fahrenheit, the physicist, left us his legacy. (See #2, **cantinflear** and #192, **carrancear**.)

- **Sayings**. These expressions of pithy wisdom are sprinkled throughout conversational speech. *The early bird gets the worm* reminds us that rising at the crack of dawn has its benefits. Likewise, every Spanish country has its own sayings, and Mexico is no exception. (See #198, **Ahogado el niño, tapado el pozo**; #251, **El que con leche se quema, hasta el jocoque sopla**; and #267, **No se puede chiflar y comer pinole**.)

- **Slang**. Yes, you will find some slang in these pages. As language evolves, today's slang may well work its way into tomorrow's textbooks. (See #3, **chirris**; #44, **¡Híjole!**; and #396, **¡Tranquis!**)

The only aspect of conversational speech we have eliminated are vulgarities. Consider this a selection for general audiences, kids included.

HOW THIS BOOK IS ORGANIZED

Unlike a dictionary, which few people read from cover to cover, this book is organized by categories, each defined by the fourteen chapter titles. In each chapter, entries are further sorted into sub-categories. This allows you to learn words, phrases, and sayings that are at least loosely related to one another. Connecting something new to what you already know is a key hook in the learning process.

After most terms, you will find the literal meaning, whether in Spanish or the language of origin. Sometimes this is based on the principal definition in the *Diccionario de la Real Academia Española*. In the case of idioms and sayings, it is a very literal word-for-word translation from Spanish to English. In many instances, such a rendering is little more than gibberish. However, knowing the literal meaning can unlock greater insights, either by comparing its meaning in standard Spanish with Mexican Spanish or by seeing the linguistic relationship. For example, term #6 **en bola** literally means *in ball*. It means doing something in a group. When we are together, we form a sort of human ball. Get the idea? Ridiculous as it may first seem, you might discover unexpected connections.

Most terms contain example sentences. Some I created, but many were pulled from the Internet—Twitter being an excellent source for colloquial Spanish, since people tend to tweet just as they would speak. Others were culled from the pages of Mexican newspapers. The term in question is set to **bold** type and its corresponding translation in English, to *italics*, as an aid to quickly identifying the word and its contextual translation. Please note that I subscribe to meaning-based translation. That means that the translations found in pairs at the bottom of each term's entry represent an effort to express the same *idea* as the original, albeit in far different literal wording. This is in stark contrast to the literal meaning of each term.

THE TONGUE THAT BURNED MY MOUTH: MEXICAN SPANISH

From 1995 to 2012 my wife and I lived in Nicaragua. There we gradually adapted to the local Spanish, learning its peculiar vocabulary, idioms, sayings, and other idiosyncrasies. In 2012, however, the organization where we volunteered transferred us to a regional office in Mexico City. That move suddenly thrust us into a completely new version of Spanish. Just as you swap your phone chip when moving to another country, it is as if we had to replace the linguistic chip in our brains.

It was clear that every Latin country speaks a very different version of Spanish. They are *divided* by a common language.

In any case, those years in Nicaragua—a lifetime for us—created a sort of Spanish language touchstone. It's as if we had generated neat folders in our minds, some with sayings, others with vocabulary, others with phrases. Together they formed a pattern, a fingerprint unique to Nicaraguan Spanish. The antivirus software on your computer works in much the same way. It continually compares new files on your machine to a database of known offenders. When a match is made to a rogue file, the software does its job, eliminating the intruder and protecting the integrity of your data, often alerting you of the near miss in ominous red type.

In this instance, whenever we would encounter words, phrases, or sayings not in our database, it's as if a red flag went up. My supervisor would revise a memorandum I had written and hand it back to me with: "*No, bájale. Estás echando mucha crema a los tacos.*" Literal translation: "No, lower it. You are putting too much cream on the tacos." Lower it? Lower what? The margins? The tone? And what did cream on tacos have to do with my memo? It didn't fit the pattern. Red flag!

In another conversation, a friend of mine was describing how astonished he was when some construction workers with simple tools were able to remove a large boulder that blocked the foundation of a new building. He gushed: "*No, cuando quitaron esa piedra, ¡hasta los ingenieros se quedaron de a seis!*" Literal translation: "When they removed that boulder, even the engineers were left at six." At six what? And why six? Why not five or seven? Red flag!

Even our files for simple vocabulary had to be amended. For me a kitchen sink was a **lavabo** or **lavamanos**. But now I heard **tarja**. Red flag! And we didn't dare take a dip in a **piscina**, or swimming pool. Here it's an **alberca**. Red flag! When I finally realized what they were talking about, someone would point out: "*Ya te cayó el veinte.*" Literal translation: "The twenty finally fell for you." What twenty? Why did it fall? What does that have to do with me??? Red flags were buzzing past my ears like the lead car at Indianapolis. The new words and phrases were jumping out at me like bullies in a dark alley.

And so we did the only thing we could: We began to write down in a little notebook all of these newfound expressions and what they really meant. We had to create another folder in our mind clearly labeled: Mexican Spanish. Instead of pretending to understand the dialogue, we unabashedly stopped it in its tracks. "Excuse me, what is that word you said? What does it mean? In what context do you use it?" And we lassoed those red flags and brought them to their knees. Now they are ours. And they can be yours too.

The Indianapolis 500 offers 500 miles of pavement around which determined drivers push their polished machines to the limit. No one wants a red flag to stop the engines from revving to the max. And we don't want red flags to stop you as you race to learn the hottest variety of Spanish on the planet: Mexican Spanish.

There are two hundred laps in Indianapolis, and this book has more than two hundred pages. Consider each page a lap, and each new term, another mile closer to your language goals.

Savor each bite. Let your mouth water. Let it burn. Just like it did ours.

I hope that you enjoy each flaming term as much as I enjoyed writing about them. After all, as a collection, they are my burning tongue.

Mouth Contents

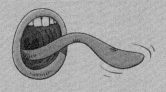

A Conversation Piece

AMOUNTS

A REVENTAR
LITERAL MEANING: TO THE POINT OF BURSTING

EVER been to a party with standing room only? Then you can identify with this idiom which means *to be packed in*.

¿Fuiste al antro anoche? El lugar estaba **a reventar**.

Did you go to the nightclub last night? The place was *bursting at the seams*.

CANTINFLEAR
LITERAL MEANING: TO SPEAK LIKE CANTINFLAS

CANTINFLAS was the stage name for one of Mexico's most beloved comics, Mario Moreno. He was famous for chatting ad nauseum without saying anything at all, and he wasn't even a politician. His character morphed into a verb that glorifies verbosity.

¡Deje de **cantinflear**!

Get to the point!

CHIRRIS
LITERAL MEANING: UNUSUAL ABBREVIATION OF CHIQUITO, SMALL

WANT to sound upscale? This is part of the vocabulary of the social elite— or the wannabees.

① Sírveme un **chirris** de whiskey.
Serve me *just a little* whiskey.

② Ese coche es demasiado **chirris** para mí.
That car is too *tiny* for me.

See also #259, **fresa**.

DE PLANO
LITERAL MEANING: OF FLAT

HERE'S an idiom you will hear daily. It means *completely* or *totally*, different from the standard Spanish **completamente**.

> Ese tipo **de plano** está loco.
>
> That guy is *completely* crazy.

DE TOCHO MOROCHO
LITERAL MEANING: OF EVERYTHING A LITTLE

VARIETY is the spice of life. Choose this phrase when you need a little bit of everything.

> Elena entró en la panadería y compró **de tocho morocho**.
>
> Elena went into the bakery and bought *a little bit of everything*.

EN BOLA
LITERAL MEANING: IN BALL

IF you are a social person, you especially enjoy going out in larger groups. When Mexicans go out **en bola**, they are going out with the whole gang.

> Fuimos **en bola** a ver la nueva peli.
>
> *A whole group* of us went to see the new movie.

HARTO
LITERAL MEANING: FED-UP

WHEN we have had enough of something, the amount of frustration has reached its boiling point. In standard Spanish this term means to be *fed up*. However, locals have applied it to a lot of anything. You will hear this unorthodox usage especially in the southern part of the country.

Mi patrón tiene **harto** dinero.
My boss has *loads* of money.

② Hace **harto** frío.
It's *really* cold.

8

HAY PA' AVENTAR PA' ARRIBA.
LITERAL MEANING: THERE IS [ENOUGH] TO THROW UPWARDS.

THE airspace above your home or workplace is infinite. Suppose you were to begin tossing some of your belongings skyward. When would it fill up? Never! That's the idea behind this clever local saying. If you have an excess of something, then the sky's the limit.

Después de la boda, todos nuestros amigos nos mandaron las fotos que sacaron. Ahora **hay pa' aventar pa' arriba**.

After the wedding, all of our friends sent us the pictures they took. Now we've got pictures *coming out of our noses.*

9

TANTITO
LITERAL MEANING: A LITTLE AS MUCH

CONVERSATIONAL speech seldom follows grammatical conventions. Technically speaking, **tanto** can be an adverb, an adjective or a pronoun, according to the good folks at the *Real Academia Española*, the august body that has the final word on proper Spanish. One acceptable usage, for example, would be: No tengo **tanto** tiempo como Roberto. This translate to: I don't have *as much* time as Roberto. However, in Mexico **tanto** in its diminutive form has come to mean *a little bit*. Don't tell the Royal Academy.

① Regálame **tantita** azúcar, porfa.
Could you give me *a little* sugar, please?

② Espéreme **tantito**, por favor.
Wait *just a moment* please.

As seen in these examples, **tantito** is polite and often combined with requests.

TITIPUCHAL

LITERAL MEANING: BLACK DIRT OR SAND

NOW what? Actually, it is Nahuatl. As is the case of many terms in this volume, this word comes from the Aztecs' native language—from *tlallic,* black thing, and *putzalli,* dirt or a lot of sand. Of course, they were not the first to equate sand grains with multitudes of people. In Bible times, Abraham was promised that his offspring would be like the sands of the sea. **Titipuchal** embraces that same notion.

> A: ¿Cómo te fue en la tienda?
>
> B: ¡No! ¡Hubieras visto el **titipuchal** de gente!
>
> A: How did it go at the store?
>
> B: You should have seen it! *Everyone and his mother* were there!

TODA LA RAZA

LITERAL MEANING: THE WHOLE RACE

HOW many people have the same race as you? Surely millions, if not billions. This hyperbolic phrase claims as much.

> ¡Llevé todo el santo día verificando mi coche porque llegó **toda la raza**!
>
> It took me the whole stinkin' day to do my emissions test because *every Tom, Dick, and Harry* showed up!

CLARITY

AGARRAR LA ONDA

LITERAL MEANING: TO GRAB THE WAVE

SINCE conversation ebbs and flows, it is much like the waves of the sea. Do you get my drift? To understand, you have to catch the wave.

Traté de explicar al jefe mi ausencia, pero no me **agarró la onda**.

I tried to explain my absence to my boss, but he didn't *get my drift*.

REBORÚJAMELO MÁS DESPACIO.

LITERAL MEANING: CONFUSE IT TO ME MORE SLOWLY.

NORTHERN Mexico is known for its flour tortillas and its people, for their dry humor, as arid as the surrounding desert. As a case in point, this sarcastic phrase originates in Chihuahua. There, **reborujado** means *confusing* and the verb **reborujar**, *to confuse*. Try this. If you visit Chihuahua and someone sputters to you with a velocity that renders them unintelligible, just say this:

① Disculpe, **reborújamelo más despacio**.

I'm sorry. *Could you confuse me a little more slowly?*

② Mi primo habla todo **reborujado**; No le entiendo.

Mi cousin *babbles away*; I can't understand him.

SHILE SHILACA, A OSHO OSHENTA EL KILO

If you visit Chihuahua, you will quickly notice that the locals pronounce their *ch*'s as *sh*'s. The headline above should actually read: **Chile chilaca, a ocho ochenta el kilo**. Hence, **mushashos**, play along. See also #321, ¡**Ay, Chihuahua**!.

CONFIDENTIALITY

BALCONEAR

LITERAL MEANING: TO BE BALCONIED

IF you were on a balcony, it would be difficult to hide. You would be squarely in the public eye. On the other hand, an observer on a balcony could see what you are doing and spread the word. Either way, this verb speaks of a snitch.

En la fiesta del domingo sus amigas la **balconearon** con todas sus indiscreciones.

At Sunday's party, her friends *aired her dirty laundry*, all the indiscretions.

NO CHISTES NADA; HAY PÁJAROS EN EL ALAMBRE.

LITERAL MEANING: DON'T SAY ANYTHING; THERE ARE BIRDS ON THE WIRE.

EVER heard a juicy tidbit thanks to a "little birdy"? If so, you will get the gist of this phrase. Don't be confused with the verb **chistar**. It has nothing to do with jokes, or **chistes**. Rather, it means *to not say a word*. The entire phrase could be translated: Don't say a word. A little birdie might hear you.

① No **chisté** nada.
I didn't say a word.

② El niño fue a la escuela sin **chistar**.
The boy went to school without *complaint*.

DESCRIPTION

ASÍ Y ASADO

LITERAL MEANING: THIS WAY AND GRILLED

WE humans like to play with words. During the COVID-19 pandemic, some started to call those who took no precautions *covidiots*. And it stuck. This phrase was born from **así o asá**, *like this or like that*.

No seas **así y asado**.

Don't be *like that*.

CON SANTO Y SEÑA

LITERAL MEANING: WITH SAINT AND SIGN

THE book *De dónde viene* by Arturo Ortega de Morán explains that in ancient military battles, some soldiers died by friendly fire, especially at night when it was not clear who was approaching. To remedy this, armies learned to ask for a name, which was a code only they knew. In time this name was called a

santo. Later, a sign, or **seña** was added, much like modern two-factor verification.

Me explicó lo que sucedió en el accidente **con santo y seña**.

He told me what happened in the accident, *down to the last detail*.

DOUBT

¿A POCO?

LITERAL MEANING: A LITTLE?

WANT to really sound Mexican? Then ask this question after every piece of information received.

A: ¿Escuchaste que María está encinta?

A: Did you hear that María is pregnant?

B: **¿A poco?**

B: *No! Really?*

CHECAR

LITERAL MEANING: TO CHECK

IMPORTED straight from the USA and the English word *check*, this is a departure from the standard Spanish **revisar**.

¿Ya **checaste** tu correo electrónico?

Did you already *check* your email?

DIZQUE

LITERAL MEANING: SAYS THAT

THIS is short for **dice que**, that is, he says or she says.

Fui al **dizque** médico, pero no me ayudó para nada.

I went to that *supposed* doctor, but he didn't help me at all.

21

¡MANDE!

LITERAL MEANING: GIVE THE ORDER!

SOME foreigners take offense at this term. They view it as a relic of the servitude imposed during the Spanish conquest. Nevertheless, scholars who have scoured documents from the past 500 years find no support for such theories. In either case, to this day in Mexican Spanish this is the most natural and polite response when you didn't catch what was said.

¡**Mande!** No te oí.

Excuse me. I didn't hear you.

22

NO ES LO MISMO QUE LO MESMO.

LITERAL MEANING: THE SAME IS NOT THE SEME [SIC].

IN rural Mexico, some mispronounce **mismo** as **mesmo**. This saying is akin to: *Compare apples to apples.* Protest with this when you doubt the parallelism.

23

SEPA LA BOLA.

LITERAL MEANING: MAY THE BALL KNOW.

SEPA is the third-person subjective form of **saber**, to know. The verb mood casts doubt; the "ball" refers to the people.

A: ¿A qué hora es la reunión? A: What time is the meeting?
B: **Sepa la bola.**   B: *Who knows?*

24

SIEMPRE NO

LITERAL MEANING: ALWAYS NO

EVER known people to change their minds? It happens all the time.

Yo iba a jugar al parque, pero ahora mi mamá dice que **siempre no**.

I was going to play at the park, but now my mom *in the end said no.*

EXAGGERATION

¡BÁJALE!

LITERAL MEANING: LOWER IT!

AS far as intensity is concerned, you can step it up a notch or lower it one. This command encourages the latter. Note the following blog headline:

Bájale, Nostradamus. Es falso que haya epidemias cada 100 años.

Not so fast, Nostradamus. It's not true that there are epidemics every 100 years.

NI YENDO A BAILAR A CHALMA

LITERAL MEANING: NOT EVEN BY GOING TO DANCE AT CHALMA

CHALMA is a town in the State of Mexico where pilgrims trek and perform a ritual dance in hopes of getting a miracle.

No te van a dar el préstamo, **ni yendo a bailar a Chalma**.

You're not getting the loan; *it would take a miracle*.

FREQUENCY

A MORIR

LITERAL MEANING: GOING TO DIE

WE are born, we grow up, we have children, we grow old and die. From the perspective of many, death is the ultimate end. When Mexicans do something **a morir**, they do so frequently or in exaggerated amounts.

① Cómete todo lo que quieras. Hay tacos **a morir**.
   Eat all you want. We have *boatloads* of tacos.

② Le echó salsa **a morir** en su comida.
   He heaped *tons of* salsa on his food.

Feel free to say **a morir** all you wish. It won't kill you.

28

LUEGO LUEGO

LITERAL MEANING: THEN THEN

DUPLICATED words often take on a life of their own. *So* is not the same as *so-so*. This twin phrase means *right away* and has a sense of urgency to it.

¿Quieres que vaya **luego luego**?

Do you want me to go *right now*?

Compare with #66, **ahorita**.

29

PALABRAS DOMINGUERAS

LITERAL MEANING: SUNDAY WORDS

ONCE upon a time, Sundays were for church. Remember that for decades mass was held in Catholic Mexico in Latin, a language unknown to parishioners. Seldom used words plucked from dictionaries now carry this label.

¡Ya deja de tus **palabras domingueras**! Háblame sencillo.

Enough of your *big words*. Talk to me plain and simple.

GENERAL

30

CHIPI CHIPI

LITERAL MEANING: DROP DROP

AN onomatopoeia is a word that sounds like what it represents, and this is an example. When light rain falls, the sound locals hear is **chipi chipi**.

A: ¿Cómo está el clima?

B: Está **chipi chipi**. (Another option: Está **chispeando**.)

A: What's the weather like?

B: It's *drizzling*.

> ## ONE SIZE FITS ALL
>
> Here's a simple trick to save hours of vocabulary learning. If you don't know or can't remember the name of an object, just say: **Páseme ese chunche**. That means: Pass me that *thingamagig*. Yes, **chunche** is a generic filler word. Its cousins are **cachivache**, **tiliche**, or in the plural **chivas**. If you are visiting the Yucatán area around Cancún, try **negociante**. Yet another option is to point to the object you want and say: **Dame desa**. Who said Spanish was hard?

EH

LITERAL MEANING: [FILLER WORD]

WE all have our word whiskers. I remember one woman who used to say "and everything" at the end of every sentence. Others scatter *er*s and *umm*s like a rogue newspaper delivery boy. In Central Mexico the **eh** adds emphasis to the spoken word. Canadian speakers, rejoice! You can transfer your **eh** from English to Spanish for no fee whatsoever.

① Está sabroso, **eh**.
That's *really* delicious.

② Gracias, **eh**.
Thanks *so much*.

EQUIS

LITERAL MEANING: THE LETTER X

REMEMBER algebra? x–5=8. The x is merely a variable, but without much character. Mexicans applied the idea to this adjective.

No voy a ir a esa fiesta **equis** con Maribel. Ella es una chava **equis**.

I'm not going to that *boring* party with Maribel. She's a *wallflower*.

POS

LITERAL MEANING: WELP

SELECT this adverb to start your sentences, and you will sound more local. Yes, the correct pronunciation is **pues**, but live a little! During the 2017

Mexico City protests, some students created #**pos**mebrinco on social media, encouraging riders to jump the turnstiles in the subway entrances.

Pos, me brinco.

Welp, I am going to hop over.

¿QUÉ PACHUCA POR TOLUCA?

LITERAL MEANING: WHAT PACHUCA-ED IN TOLUCA?

A common Spanish greeting is **¿Qué pasó?** Creative minds twisted this into the more informal **¿Qué pachó?** From there it was just one more jump to **¿Qué Pachuca por Toluca?** In this case the only relation between the two cities is that they rhyme. Consider it a loose translation of *Whaaassssssup?*

ALLÍ TIENE SU POBRE CASA.

LITERAL MEANING: THERE YOU HAVE YOUR POOR HOUSE.

ONE of the first things we ask a person we meet for the first time is where they live. After telling you the name of the town, rural folks will add this line. It's a self-deprecating offer of hospitality.

Vivo en San Juan de los Ranchos. **Allí tiene su pobre casa**.

I live in San Juan de los Ranchos. *My house isn't much, but you're welcome to it.*

BUENO

LITERAL MEANING: GOOD

HOW do you answer the phone? In most Hispanic countries it would be something like **Aló, Buenos(as) días/tardes/noches**, o maybe just **Buenas**. But not here. This is the standard greeting. If you hear nothing, it will be:

Bueno…**bueno, bueno, bueno**.

*Hello…hello…*is anyone there?

GAFETE
LITERAL MEANING: NAME TAG

WE all cherish wearing those little tags on our lapels at conferences that say: Hello, my name's Bob. And especially if your name really is Bob. Standard Spanish dubs them **tarjetas de solapa**, but here they are **gafetes**.

¡VIVITO Y COLEANDO!
LITERAL MEANING: ALIVE AND MOVING MY TAIL

INFORMAL greetings make their best attempt at humor. To change things up, choose this anthropomorphic phrase as the response to **¿Cómo estás?**

A: ¿Cómo estás?   A: How are you?

B: **¡Vivito y coleando!**   B: *Alive and kicking!*

IMAGINATION

HAZ DE CUENTA QUE...
LITERAL MEANING: MAKE OF ACCOUNT THAT...

THERE were few days at my place of employment when I did not hear this phrase. It's the standard way of saying: Imagine that...

> **Haz de cuenta que** tienes a 100 empleados y todos piden vacaciones al mismo tiempo. ¿Qué pasaría?
>
> *Imagine that* you have 100 employees and they all ask for vacation at the same time. What would happen?

THINKING INSIDE THE BOX

In English thinking outside the box is praise for creativity. But what if you stayed inside the box? Meet the Mexican phrase **de cajón**, literally *from the box*. If you are asked **preguntas de cajón**, they are *standard questions*. **Chistes de cajón** could be rendered *the same old jokes*. See also #415, **cajón**.

40

¡CHALE!

LITERAL MEANING: WOW!

SURPRISED? Annoyed? Disappointed? Saddened? Angry? Whatever the case, here's a one-size-fits-all interjection for you. Context will determine its meaning in any given sentence.

① ¡**Chale**, me estafaron!   ② ¡**Chale**, quebré mi taza de café!
Oh no! They ripped me off!   *Dang!* I broke my coffee cup!

41

¡CHANCLAS, PETRA!

LITERAL MEANING: FLIP FLOPS, PETRA!

PETRA is a woman's name, which these days sounds old-fashioned. This is yet another euphemistic exclamation of surprise. One woman tweeted:

¡**Chanclas, Petra**! Pos, habla con él y ya. ¿Cuál es la bronca?

Oh my goodness! Well, talk to him and get it over with. What's the problem?

42

¡CHISPAS!

LITERAL MEANING: SPARKS!

THIS is another interjection of surprise similar to the aforementioned ¡**Chanclas**! To add culinary variety, exclaim: ¡**Chispas de chocolate**!.

43

¡GUÁCALA!

LITERAL MEANING: DIRTY WATER CONTAINER

BEFORE indoor plumbing, how would you wash your food or dishes? Enter the **huacal**, essentially a sink with no drain. After a while that dirty water would stink and they would heave it out the window. If you get a whiff of stench, shout: ¡**Guácala**! It means: *Gross! That stinks!* See also #70, ¡**Aguas**!.

¡HÍJOLE!

LITERAL MEANING: TO THE SON!

WE hereby present you with the consummate Mexican exclamation of surprise or dismay.

① **¡Híjole!** ¡Esos son los mejores tacos!
Wow! Those are the best tacos.

② **¡Híjole!** ¡La fila está larguísima!
Yikes! The line is super long!

¡A SU MECHA!

LITERAL MEANING: TO YOUR MOPHEAD!

SPEAKING ill of another's mother is the subject of insults the world over and Mexico is no exception. Originally, the insult was **para su madre. Para** has been clipped to its last letter and **mecha** substituted for **madre.** Very few even know of its origin and it has become another form of *Wow!* Variations include **¡A su bárbaro!** and simply **¡A su!.**

NUMBERS

DOS QUE TRES

LITERAL MEANING: TWO OR THREE

WHAT'S the math here? None at all. Here's a numerical option for *so-so.*

A: ¿Cómo está tu abuelo?

B: **Dos que tres**.

A: How's your grandpa?

B: He's *tolerable.*

MAL TERCIO

LITERAL MEANING: BAD THIRD

IN English your spouse is your better half. But what is the bad third? The chaperone, of course.

Voy a la película gratis esta noche, pero como **mal tercio**.

I am going to the movie tonight for free, but unfortunately as the *chaperone*.

 48

PONERLE UN CUATRO

Literal Meaning: to put to him a four

CRITTERS generally walk on all fours, as we say. Want to catch them? Set a trap. That will help you remember the meaning of this numerical idiom.

El policía **le puso un cuatro** al ratero.

The policeman *set a trap* for the thief.

 49

QUEDARSE DE A SEIS

Literal Meaning: to end up at six

SURPRISED? Astonished? Then in Mexican Spanish you are figuratively at six. Some scholars surmise that this refers to bygone years when six-inch cannonballs blasted a surprising amount of damage. Here's another possibility: In local schools children are graded on a scale of 1–10. What is the threshold for passing? A six. Regardless of its origin, don't let this idiom catch you by surprise.

Cuando mi equipo de futbol ganó el campeonato, **me quedé de a seis**.

When my soccer team won the championship, I was *flabbergasted*.

 50

CAERLE EL VEINTE

Literal Meaning: to have the twenty fall to you

EVER make a phone call on a public telephone? Years ago in Mexico you had to put a twenty-cent coin in the machine and, when it fell, you got a dial tone.

Diez minutos después de escuchar el chiste, se echó a reír. **Le cayó el veinte**.

Ten minutes after hearing the joke, she started laughing. It finally *dawned on her*.

OPINION

51

¿CÓMO CREES?
LITERAL MEANING: HOW DO YOU BELIEVE?

MOST of the time when you hear this phrase, locals are not asking for your opinion. It is a gentle rebuff.

A: Siento que no soy inteligente.

B: ¿**Cómo crees**? ¡Eres todo un genio!

A: I feel like I'm not very smart.

B: *Get outta here*! You're a genius!

52

¿CÓMO VES?
LITERAL MEANING: HOW DO YOU SEE?

WHEN a Mexican asks you this, they aren't interested in your visual acuity.

Salgamos mañana a las seis. ¿**Cómo ves**?

Let's leave tomorrow at six. *What do you think?*

53

¿QUÉ CREES?
LITERAL MEANING: WHAT DO YOU BELIEVE?

This phrase finds its English twin in the phrase *Guess what?*.

¿**Qué crees**? Decidí siempre mudarme.

Guess what? I decided to move after all.

54

LATIRLE CHOCOLATE
LITERAL MEANING: TO BEAT CHOCOLATE

A **latido de corazón** is a heartbeat. If you like your friend's proposal, just respond with this rhyme:

Me late chocolate.

I like the idea.

REQUESTS

HAZME EL PARO.
LITERAL MEANING: MAKE THE STOP FOR ME.

HOW do you feel when you visit someone and they don't stop to listen? Betrayed. Conversely, a good friend would gladly stop everything to help.

Amigo, **hazme el paro**. Recógeme un kilo de tortilla, porfa.

Buddy, *do me a favor*. Can you pick me up a kilo of tortillas please?

LIMOSNERO Y CON GARROTE
LITERAL MEANING: BEGGAR WITH A STICK

DON'T be overly demanding when making requests, or else you will be called this. It's similar to: *Beggars can't be choosers.*

NO SEAS MALITO(A)...
LITERAL MEANING: DON'T BE MEAN...

WANT to soften your friend before launching a request? Then start with this. The implication is that if your buddy is good, he will grant your wish.

No seas malito. Préstame 200 pesos.

Don't be a meanie. Loan me 200 pesos.

OCUPAR
LITERAL MEANING: TO BE BUSY OR TO USE

IN standard Spanish **ocupado** is the word for *busy*. But Mexicans give it a new twist, as seen below.

Ocupo un martillo. ¿Tienes uno?

I *need* a hammer. Do you have one?

SHARING

 59

MÓCHATE CON...
LITERAL MEANING: CHOP YOURSELF WITH...

MOCHAR in standard Spanish is *to cut off*. And if you want to share with someone, you cut away a portion for them.

Oye, **móchate** con los churros.

Hey, *share* some of your churros with me.

In true street lingo, you might even beg: ¡**Mochilas para los cuadernos**!. The meaning is the same. See also #436, **hecho la mocha**.

 60

PONTE LA DE PUEBLA.
LITERAL MEANING: PUT ON THE ONE FROM PUEBLA.

PUEBLA'S professional soccer team sports a unique uniform design. A wide band cuts diagonally across each player's body down to the waist. If it were a knife, it would slice him in half. Consequently, this has the same meaning as the previous term, **Móchate.** If your friend has something that you would like, do this: Spread your thumb and index finger out wide and gesture cutting a diagonal swath from your shoulder to your waist. As you do so, with sad eyes implore: **Ponte la de Puebla.** We hope it works, but mileage may vary.

Carnal, **ponte la de Puebla.**

Pal, *share some of the love.*

SOCIAL STATUS

 61

GENTE BIEN
LITERAL MEANING: GOOD PEOPLE

Here's yet another expression to refer to the high-class or elite. If you change the order of the words, notice how the meaning changes:

La **gente bien** no son siempre bien gente.

High-class people aren't always very nice.

See also #259, **fresa**.

MUY ACÁ
LITERAL MEANING: VERY HERE

WHEN we say in English he is neither here nor there, it means he is of no importance. **Muy acá** is quite the opposite.

Me compré unas mezclillas **muy acá**.

I bought myself some *really hip* jeans.

NACO
LITERAL MEANING: [NAHUATL] NAKED

AT the other end of the spectrum, we have **naco**, a derogatory reference to the unrefined and crude. An indignant woman tweeted:

Qué **naco** andar contando lo que alguna vez con confianza te dijeron.

That is so *ghetto* to spread what was once told you in confidence.

SURPRISE

APANTALLAR
LITERAL MEANING: TO SCREEN

HOW did you feel when you saw your first movie on the big screen? Impressed, right? That's the premise behind this showy verb.

① La presentación del gerente general nos dejó a todos **apantallados**.
The general manager's presentation left us all *very impressed*.

② Mi papá anduvo por todo el pueblo **apantallando** a todos su nuevo coche.
My dad was going around town *showing off* big new car to everyone.

65

¡NO TE PASES!

LITERAL MEANING: DON'T PASS THROUGH!

AT first hearing this exclamation, I froze for a second. I thought I had overstepped my boundaries in some way. Here, however, it just means: *You're kidding.*

No es cierto. **¡No te pases!**

That's not true. *You're joking!*

TIME

66

AHORITA

LITERAL MEANING: LITTLE NOW

CARIBBEAN Spanish speakers have a beef with this term. For them, it means *right now*. On the other hand, the Mexican **ahorita** defies the stopwatch. It runs the gamut from just a few minutes to hours, days—or even eternity, depending on the context.

① Lo atendemos **ahorita**.
We will be with you *shortly*.

② **Ahorita** saco la basura.
I'll take out the trash *later on*.

For contrast, see also #28, **luego luego**.

67

DAR LARGAS

LITERAL MEANING: GIVE LONGS

IF only I could get around to procrastinating. Sigh. When a project gets postponed repeatedly, perhaps deliberately, **dar largas** fits the bill. The newspaper *El Heraldo* had the following headline:

Evita **dar largas** a un amor malsano

Avoid *dragging out* an unhealthy relationship

DE VOLADA

LITERAL MEANING: OF FLOWN

TIME flies, at least in this fleet idiom. If you need it done right away, **ahorita** won't cut it. Specify that it needs to be completed **de volada**.

Necesito que me traigas el pedido **de volada**.

I need you to bring me the order *on the double*.

ORA SÍ

LITERAL MEANING: NOW YES

THIS is the shortened version of **ahora sí**. It may announce an imminent consequence of our actions or a resolution to begin anew.

① Viene el patrón. **Ora sí** te va a despedir.
The boss is coming. *This time* he's *really* going to fire you.

② **Ora sí** nos vamos a poner los tapabocas cuando andamos en la calle.
Now we're determined to wear our masks when we walk in the streets.

WARNINGS

¡AGUAS!

LITERAL MEANING: WATERS!

NEVER take the humble toilet for granted. Back in the old days, you would have to do your business in a primitive container and then dump the unsavory contents out the window. As a courtesy, just before dropping the bomb, a Spanish speaker would yell out: **¡Aguas!** The feared waters were coming! Today it just means: *Watch out!* When driving a vehicle, you might exhort your copilot:

Échame aguas.

Tell me if anything's coming.

OUT OF ORDER

There are certain elements of Mexican Spanish with unusual syntax, that is, a curious word order. You may hear people say: **Deja checo**. (Let me check.) Normally, this would be **Déjame checar**. Also, the pronoun **su** means *his*, *her*, or *your*. Due to the possible ambiguity, instead of saying **su mamá**, in everyday speech you will often hear **su mamá de ella**, which sounds like overkill to Spanish speakers from elsewhere. Usually, the antecedent of **su** can be deduced by context.

CON TIENTO

LITERAL MEANING: WITH SENSE OF TOUCH

NOT everyone can walk on eggshells. That would require extraordinary finesse. That's what's captured in this phrase.

Como Manuela está grave en el hospital, hay que informarle de la muerte de su hermana **con mucho tiento**.

Since Manuela is in serious condition in the hospital, you have to break the news of her sister's death *very delicately*.

MÁS TE VALE.

LITERAL MEANING: IT'S MORE WORTH IT TO YOU.

NEED to give advice to someone? Add this to your arsenal.

Va a llover por la tarde. **Más te vale** llevar una sombrilla.

It's going to rain this afternoon. You *had better* take an umbrella.

Animals on the Loose.

BEASTS OF BURDEN

COMO CABALLO LECHERO
LITERAL MEANING: LIKE A DAIRY HORSE

PITY the poor horse at the dairy. He had to get up before the crack of dawn and haul huge containers of milk all day. What kind of velocity would he muster? Barely a snail's pace.

> ¿Qué pasó, Enrique? Andas **como caballo lechero**.

> What happened, Enrique? You're *slower than cold molasses in January*.

ENTRE MENOS BURROS, MÁS OLOTES.
LITERAL MEANING: THE FEWER THE DONKEYS, THE MORE CORN COBS.

DID fewer guests than expected show up at your dinner party? Don't fret. Look at the bright side. *There's more for everyone else.* That's the basis for this barnyard wisdom. If your party of twelve just became a party of eight, fire off this optimistic adage—even if it is a little corny.

> A: No vinieron los Vargas.

> B: **Entre menos burros, más olotes**.

> A: The Vargas family didn't show up.

> B: *Great! There's more for us.*

ENTRE MULA Y MULA
NOMÁS LAS PATADAS SE OYEN.
LITERAL MEANING: BETWEEN MULES ONLY THE KICKS ARE HEARD.

MULES aren't known for their reasonableness. What if two stubborn beasts were to meet head on and neither yielded? Sparks will fly. Or, according to this saying, only kicks will be heard. When two hard-headed colleagues are at odds, apply this saying. It's similar to *It looks like they've met their match*, but heavier on the obstinacy.

SI TE DIGO QUE LA BURRA ES PARDA, ES PORQUE TRAIGO LOS PELOS EN LA MANO.

LITERAL MEANING: IF I TELL YOU THE DONKEY IS BROWN, IT'S BECAUSE I HAVE THE HAIRS IN MY HAND.

WHY should I believe you? Because of your looks? Just because you say so? No, I want evidence. If your workmates or schoolmates question your arguments, just smile and say this. It's akin to: *I've got the smoking gun.* Just make sure that you actually *do* have that smoking gun.

DON'T LET THEM KILL YOUR ROOSTER

If it turns out that those donkey hairs weren't actually as brown as you expected, then you will put another barnyard animal in harm's way, the poor rooster. Why? Because you will swallow your pride and concede: **Me mataron el gallo**. That literally means that they killed your rooster—your argument.

BIRDS

SE CREE LA DIVINA GARZA.

LITERAL MEANING: HE THINKS HE'S THE DIVINE HERON.

EVER met someone who thought they were God's gift, better than everyone else? Mexican actress María Félix once boasted:

Yo no **me creo la divina garza**; soy la divina garza.
I don't think I'm God's gift; I am God's gift.

SE ME HACE MUY OJONA PARA SER PALOMA.

LITERAL MEANING: ITS EYES ARE TOO BIG TO BE A DOVE.

DOES that tantalizing sales pitch sound too good to be true? Then reply with this avian saying to let the salesman know you weren't born yesterday.

TECOLOTE

MEET the local term for *owl*, different from the standard Spanish **búho**. This nocturnal bird frequently has its eyes wide open. Perhaps for this reason this term is informally applied to police officers or night watchmen.

Ese **tecolocote** es bien gente; de noche siempre me acompaña hasta la puerta.

That *night watchman* is super nice; at night he walks me all the way to my door.

BUGS

CHAPULÍN

READY to try some exotic food? Savor these tasty critters. **Chapulín** is the Nahuatl-derived name for the *grasshopper*. **El chapulín colorado**, or Red Grasshopper, was the popular 70's TV show which parodied superheroes.

> ### CHAPULTEPEC—A HOP, SKIP, AND JUMP AWAY
> Chapultepec Park is the emerald jewel of Mexico City. There you can visit the iconic **Museo de Antropología** as well as the opulent **Castillo de Chapultepec**. As you enjoy the sights, just remember that the name itself comes from the same root as the term above. In Nahuatl it means *Grasshopper Hill*.

COLOR DE HORMIGA
LITERAL MEANING: COLOR OF ANT

EVER been to a red zone? In Spanish a **zona roja** refers to a dangerous area of town. In the NFL, when a team advances to the red zone, it is within the opponent's 20-yard line; it means they are in danger of scoring. Since some ants are a reddish color, when a situation becomes ant-color, watch out! Notice this headline from *El Diario de Coahuila*:

Podría ponerse **color de hormiga** la economía

Economy could be *in jeopardy*

PELÓN Y CON PIOJOS

LITERAL MEANING: BALD AND WITH LICE

IMAGINE the scene: A bald man enters the doctor's office and complains:

"Doc, I need something for a lice problem."

"Lice?" responds the physician. "You don't even have hair!"

"But I *know* I have lice!" the patient retorts.

The real problem? The man is too hard to please. After a *Sol de Nayarit* piece about a Brazilian model who died during plastic surgery, a reader posted:

Eso es desafiar al Eterno…del marido **pelón y con piojos**.

That is to defy God…and from an *overly demanding* husband.

See also #56, **limosnero y con garrote**.

POR SI LAS FLAIS

LITERAL MEANING: JUST IN CASE OF FLIES

In Spanish you can punctuate a suggestion with **por si las moscas**, meaning *just in case*. Mexico's proximity to the US prompts it to anglicize the word for the pest while maintaining Spanish spelling.

Traiga una sombrilla **por si las flais**.

Bring an umbrella *just in case*.

VOLVERSE OJO DE HORMIGA

LITERAL MEANING: TO BECOME AN ANT EYE

FANCY performing an eye exam on an ant? With those minuscule eyeballs you would need a microscope. In Mexican Spanish, when someone becomes an ant's eye, it means they disappear. One man posted to YouTube:

Se volvió ojo de hormiga la mujer que tanto quería.

The woman that he so loved *hit the road*.

CATS

85

ME AGARRÓ COMO EL TIGRE DE SANTA JULIA.

LITERAL MEANING: YOU CAUGHT ME LIKE THE TIGER FROM SANTA JULIA.

SANTA JULIA was formerly a neighborhood in Mexico City, now a part of the Miguel Alemán Delegation. Its most notorious resident was a certain José de Jesús Negrete Medina, nicknamed **El Tigre**. After a life of crime, he was finally captured in 1906 while he was defecating in a cactus field. Practical usage? If you happen to be in the bathroom when your phone rings *and* it is someone with whom you are very familiar, just answer with:

Amigo, **me agarraste como El Tigre de Santa Julia**. ¿Te devuelvo la llamada?

Hey, buddy. *I'm actually on the pot.* Can I call you back?

86

DAR EL GATAZO
LITERAL MEANING: TO GIVE THE CAT SLAP

ACCORDING to an article on the website for IMER, the Mexican Radio Institute, this phrase is a derivative of **dar gato por liebre**. In most Spanish-speaking countries, this saying is applied when a salesman gives us the switcheroo and sells us inferior goods. Mexicans took the **gato** from the phrase to form this phrasal verb, which means *to look like*.

No es nuevo, pero **da el gatazo**.

It's not new, but *it could pass* for it.

87

DARLE UNA MANITA DE GATO
LITERAL MEANING: TO GIVE HIM A LITTLE CAT PAW

IF you had to write a grooming manual for cats, it might read: "Lick paw. Comb fur with paw. Repeat." What an amazing, effective method for purr-sonal hygiene! This idiom applies to any kind of touch-up.

① Laura se fue al baño para **darse una manita de gato**.
Laura went to the ladies' room *to powder her face*.

② Esta tarde voy a **darle una manita de gato** a mi cochera.
This afternoon I'm going to give my garage *a light cleaning*.

88

ES LA MISMA GATA, PERO REVOLCADA.
LITERAL MEANING: IT'S THE SAME CAT, BUT UPSIDE DOWN.

SALESMEN ply their trade trying to convince us that their product is in some way superior to that of competitors. But when the moment of truth arrives, it is often the same old thing. That's the premise for this feline saying.

Cambié a otra compañía de telefonía para ver si ahorraba dinero. Pero al final **era la misma gata, pero revolcada**.

I changed to another telephone company to see if I could save money. But in the end *it was the same old thing*.

89

UN OJO AL GATO, Y EL OTRO, AL GARABATO.
LITERAL MEANING: ONE EYE ON THE CAT, AND THE OTHER, ON THE MEATHOOK.

IMAGINE the scene at home in the kitchen back in our grandparents' day. There's no refrigeration. The meat hangs from above on a hook, called a **garabato,** thus out of the reach of rodents. But watch out for the family cat! An agile leap could be the end of the family meal. This saying is a call to alertness. Mexico's National Center for Disaster Prevention (CENAPRED) posted the following headline:

Frente al coronavirus, **un ojo al gato y otro al garabato** en la inestabilidad de laderas

Watch out for the coronavirus *and* possible landslides

47

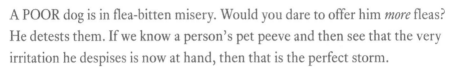

DOGS

 90

PARA SUS PULGAS

LITERAL MEANING: FOR HIS FLEAS

A POOR dog is in flea-bitten misery. Would you dare to offer him *more* fleas? He detests them. If we know a person's pet peeve and then see that the very irritation he despises is now at hand, then that is the perfect storm.

Para sus pulgas…A Felipe le sirvieron un gran plato de menudo. [Lo detesta.]

You know how he is. They served Felipe a bowl of tripe soup.

[He hates tripe soup.]

 91

QUEDARSE COMO EL PERRO DE LAS DOS TORTAS

LITERAL MEANING: TO END UP LIKE THE DOG WITH TWO SANDWICHES

WHAT a dilemma! A dog loiters just in front of a stand where **tortas**, hoagie-like sandwiches, are sold. Suddenly, a stroke of fortune comes his way when two **tortas** fall to the ground. Upon which of the two does he pounce? This one? That one? This one? Before he decides, other animals rush in for the steal; he is left with nothing. This saying is applied when indecision and perhaps a little greed leave us empty-handed.

Pedro comenzó a noviar con Ariana y Selena al mismo tiempo. ¡Pobrecito!

Quedó como el perro de las dos tortas.

Pedro started dated Ariana and Selena at the same time. The poor guy

ended up with neither one!

HAVE YOUR CAKE AND EAT IT TOO

To do so, use the right lingo. Remember that **torta** in Mexico is not cake, but rather, the tasty sandwiches mentioned above. If cake is what you desire, ask for a **pastel**. Be sure, however, not to ask for **bizcocho**. Locally, it's a vulgarity. Oops!

GOATS

¡A LAS REJAS CON TODO Y CHIVAS!

LITERAL MEANING: TO THE JAIL BARS WITH ALL AND GOATS!

WHEN individuals we trust are exposed as thieves or worse, we're indignant. Here, the **rejas,** or bars, represent the jail, and the **chivas,** their belongings.

1. Ese señor me robó todos mis ahorros. **¡A las rejas con todo y chivas!**
   That man stole all my savings. *Good riddance!*

In most references, though, it refers to all of a person's belongings.

2. Mi tío se mudó a Guadalajara **a las rejas con todo y chivas**.
   My uncle moved to Guadalajara *lock, stock, and barrel.*

CHIVEARSE

LITERAL MEANING: to make like a goat

GOATS are happiest aloof, left to themselves. When we are ashamed, we feel the same. Choose this verb when embarrassment overtakes someone.

Cuando me di cuenta que había dado todo el discurso con un frijolazo
en los dientes, **me chiveé**.

When I realized that I had given the entire speech with a piece of bean
stuck between my teeth, *I was so embarrassed.*

ÍRSELE LAS CABRAS AL MONTE

LITERAL MEANING: TO HAVE THE GOATS RUN OFF INTO THE BRUSH

DESPITE our best efforts, we may lose control of a given situation, just as a distracted shepherd might suddenly realize that his goats have run off. When that happens, you might offer the following apology:

Disculpe, **se me fueron las cabras al monte**.

I'm sorry. *Things just got away from me.*

PIGS

AQUÍ SOLO MIS CHICHARRONES TRUENAN.

LITERAL MEANING: HERE ONLY MY PORK RINDS THUNDER.

PICTURE yourself back in the day, ready for the family meal. On the menu is **chicharrón**, or pork rinds. Who gets first dibs? The father, of course. He selects the largest and crunchiest piece. When he tears it in two, according to this saying, it thunders. Nothing captures macho authority better than this. It means: *I am the only one in charge here.*

DID YOU MAKE IT THUNDER?

Although **tronar** in Spanish generally means *to thunder*, Mexicans use it in another sense as well. If someone asks you if the copier is working, you might respond with: **No, ya tronó**. That means: *No, it's broken*.

BUSCARLE RUIDO AL CHICHARRÓN

LITERAL MEANING: TO LOOK FOR SOUND IN THE PORK RIND

CONSIDERING the thunderous sound that pork rinds produce when snapped, would it be difficult to spot where the noise was coming from? You might hear the following friendly advice:

No le busques ruido al chicharrón.

Don't go looking for problems.

MAL DE PUERCO

LITERAL MEANING: BADNESS OF PIG

IT'S two o'clock in the afternoon and you've just feasted on **tacos al pastor**. How alert and energetic will you be? It's more likely that you'll take a snooze.

Después de esa comida pesada, ya me está dando el **mal de puerco**.

After that heavy lunch, I am *feeling super sleepy*.

POULTRY

CALENTURA DE POLLO

LITERAL MEANING: CHICKEN FEVER

HAVE you ever called in sick? What did you have? The flu? Barely a trickle of runny nose? A sprained eyelash? If your superiors don't believe you, then they will surmise that you are suffering from this.

Juanito llamó y dijo que estaba enfermo. Pero yo creo que lo que tiene
es **calentura de pollo**.

Juanito called in sick. But I think *he's faking it*.

DORMÍRSELE EL GALLO

LITERAL MEANING: TO HAVE YOUR ROOSTER
FALL ASLEEP ON YOU

MISSED opportunities are a shame—even for roosters!

Le dije a mi marido que los boletos a Nueva York estaban a mitad de precio,
pero **se le durmió el gallo**.

I told my husband that tickets to New York were half price, but *you snooze, you lose.*

GUAJOLOTE

MEET the local word for *turkey*, which differs from the standard **pavo**.

En la finca de mi abuelo se criaban **guajolotes**.

On my grandpa's farm they raised *turkeys*.

THE FATTENED FEMALE

Ready for a carbohydrate overload? Then try a **guajolota**. No, it's not the female turkey. This tamale-stuffed bread roll will send your blood sugar spiking. If you get addicted to them, no problem. Just quit cold turkey.

HACERSE PATO
LITERAL MEANING: TO MAKE LIKE A DUCK

WHEN have you ever seen a busy duck? Sure, they spend hour after hour paddling around in the water, but what do they ever accomplish? If someone is not working their fair share, this idiom should fit the bill.

Manuel solo **se hace pato**. Dígale que trabaje.

Manuel is *slacking off*. Tell him to work.

ME CANSO, GANSO.
LITERAL MEANING: I'M TIRED, GOOSE.

TO understand the real meaning of this phrase we must go back to the 1947 movie *El niño perdido*, which starred the Mexican comic Germán Valdés, better known as Tin Tan. In poetic humor, Tin Tan attributes the above quote to a poor mosquito. Why was he so tired? He wasn't able to fly because he sprained his foot, had a knot in the other, contracted hoof-and-mouth disease, and even went mute. The moral of the story? Against all odds, the little mosquito never gave up. It's a narrative similar to *The Little Engine that Could*. The current president of the country recently promised:

En tres años, **me canso, ganso**, estará funcionando el nuevo aeropuerto internacional.

In three years, *against all odds*, Mexico's new international airport will be operating.

Maybe he could have simply stated: "I think I can. I think I can."

PELAR GALLO
LITERAL MEANING: TO PEEL ROOSTER

YOU'VE just cut the rooster's head off. Now it's time to pluck the feathers. Will you wait until tomorrow? Of course not. It needs to be done quickly. For that reason, **pelar gallo** speaks of a fast getaway.

Al escuchar sonar la alarma, los rateros **pelaron gallo**.

When the thieves heard the alarm, they *hit the road*.

SENTIRSE LA MAMÁ DE LOS POLLITOS

LITERAL MEANING: TO FEEL LIKE THE LITTLE CHICKENS' MAMA

THERE may be a dozen little chicks waddling about the yard, yet they have but one mother. They are the followers; she is their unquestioned leader. Apply this metaphor to the female who thinks too much of herself. One woman tweeted:

> **Se siente la mamá de los pollitos** con 20k amigos en Facebook. ¿A cuántos de ellos conoce realmente?

> *She thinks she's hot snot on a rock* with 20k friends on Facebook. How many of them does she even know?

RABBITS

¡A VER TUS CONEJOS!

LITERAL MEANING: LET'S SEE YOUR RABBITS!

IF at a gym you are asked to show your six-pack, it's not likely you'll crack open a cold one. You'll expose the chiseled muscles in your abdomen. Similarly, when a Mexican asks to see your rabbits, he's really talking about your biceps. Want to make rabbits reproduce? Start pumping iron.

REPTILES & AMPHIBIANS

DEJAR LA VÍBORA CHILLANDO

LITERAL MEANING: TO LEAVE THE SNAKE CRYING

JUST the sight of a snake would send many into panic. If that snake were to stick around crying, it would draw even more attention to itself.

> Es un acto cobarde irte y **dejar la víbora chillando**.

> It is a cowardly act *to stir up trouble and then leave.*

1 07

DI RANA, Y YO SALTO.

LITERAL MEANING: SAY FROG, AND I WILL JUMP.

DO you jump at the chance to be helpful and please others? Then add this amphibian phrase to your repertoire. It is the equivalent of: *You say 'Jump' and I say, 'How high?'.*

 1 08

HACER LAGARTIJAS

LITERAL MEANING: TO DO LIZARD THINGS

LIZARDS bend their bodies laterally as they scuttle across surfaces. As you build your rabbits (see term #105), you might as well perform some of these.

A ver, muchachos. ¡Todos, a **hacer 100 lagartijas**!

OK, boys. Everybody, let's *do 100 push-ups*!

 1 09

SABER DE QUÉ LADO MASCA LA IGUANA

LITERAL MEANING: TO KNOW ON WHAT SIDE [OF THE MOUTH] THE IGUANA CHEWS

YOU would need a powerful zoom to even venture a guess as to which side of its mouth an iguana is chewing. That would be quite a lesson.

¿Eres bueno? Ven a jugar conmigo y te mostraré **de qué lado masca la iguana**.

You're good? Come play with me and *we will see what happens!*

RODENTS

---

 1 10

CHILLARSE LA ARDILLA

LITERAL MEANING: THE SQUIRREL CRIES TO ITSELF

BODY odor is enough to make any unfortunate soul cry.

Más vale ponerte desodorante. **Te chilla la ardilla**.

You had better put on some deodorant. *You've got B.O.*

RATÓN DE BIBLIOTECA

LITERAL MEANING:
THE LIBRARY MOUSE

WHO is always present at the local library? The mouse, of course.

Ese Ramón es **ratón de bibliotec**a. Se la pasa estudiando.

That Ramón is a real *bookworm*. He spends all his time studying.

WILD

CHANGO

MEET the national word for *monkey*. Even so, in certain contexts it is applied derogatorily to people. Note the following saying:

Cada chango a su mecate. (Literally, every monkey to his string.)

Mind your own business.

COYOTE

YES, this is a coyote just like in English. But it's also the term for illegal guides who charge exorbitant sums to lead people across the border into the United States. Locals also dub them **polleros**, literally *chicken handlers*.

El **coyote** quería cobrarme diez mil dólares para llevarme a los Estados.

The *smuggler* wanted to charge me ten thousand dollars to take me to the US.

THE DELICIOUS FEMALE COYOTE

Don't worry. The **coyota** is 100% vegetarian. It's a typical round pastry with sugar cane filling that you can try when you visit Sonora, Sinaloa, or parts of Baja California. So go wild. Try a **coyota.**

DAR OSO
LITERAL MEANING: TO GIVE BEAR

AT least some bears have been known to go into hibernation. When we are embarrassed, we cannot disappear from the public eye long enough. One young woman tweeted:

> Ora sí le voy a poner ganas a hacer cardio porque ya **me dio oso** mi cuerpo con tantas morras flacas y preciosas en Instagram.

> Now I'm more resolved than ever to hit the cardio because I feel *ashamed* of my body after seeing so many skinny and beautiful girls on Instagram.

ECHARSE UN COYOTITO
LITERAL MEANING: TO THROW A LITTLE COYOTE

CURLED into a ball, the sleeping coyote is the poster child for shut-eye bliss. Feel like nodding off? Just announce:

> Voy a **echarme un coyotito**.

> I am going *to take a nap*.

Another option is **echarse una pestañita**, literally *to throw a little eyelash*.

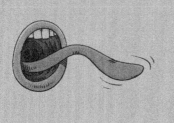

Busy Bodies

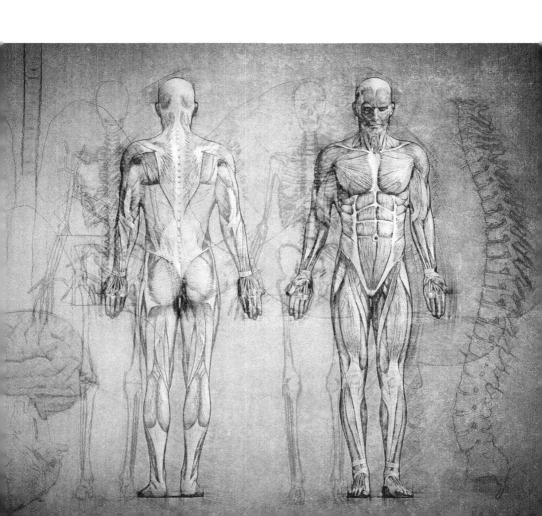

BONES

DE HUESO COLORADO

LITERAL MEANING: OF RED BONE

ARE you a die-hard? If so, this phrase may be applied to you. Your fervor is so great, it is as if your bones are burning red-hot.

> Mi tía es católica **de hueso colorado**.
>
> My aunt is a *staunch* Catholic.

CHEEKS

CACHETEANDO LAS BANQUETAS

LITERAL MEANING: SLAPPING THE SIDEWALKS WITH YOUR CHEEKS

LOVE has the power to make us crazy. Our jump for joy is so intense, it is as if on landing the g-forces stretch our cheeks all the way to the sidewalk beneath. This idiom combines two examples of local Spanish: **cachetes** for *cheeks* instead of the standard **mejillas**, and **banqueta** for *sidewalk* instead of **acera**, **andén** or other terms.

> Julio **está chacheteando las banquetas** por su novia.
>
> Julio is *head over heels in love* with his girlfriend.

CACHETÓN

LITERAL MEANING: BIG-CHEEKED

HAVING a hard time laying off those enchiladas? Bad news! You may be described as this.

No había visto a Miguel en años; se puso bien **cachetón**.

I hadn't seen Miguel in years; he's really *put on some weight*.

CHAPETEADO

LITERAL MEANING: COVERED WITH METAL SHEETING

ARE you of ruddy complexion? Then Mexicans will describe you as **chapeteado**. And don't get embarrassed, or they may say to you:

Te estás poniendo **chapeteado**.

Your *cheeks are turning red*.

CLOTHING

AGUJETAS

LITERAL MEANING: LITTLE NEEDLES

EVER thread a needle? When buying new shoes we are tasked with something similar: lacing the shoestrings. Since **aguja** in Spanish is *needle*, here the "little needles" are the shoelaces, especially for tennis shoes.

Amárrate bien las **agujetas**; si no, te va a dar un ranazo.

Tie your *shoelaces* well; if not, you'll going to fall and hurt yourself.

BICHI

EL Monumento al Pescador, or Fisherman's Monument, juts out of the sand along the seafront in Mazatlán. Naked figures of a fisherman, a woman, and marine life pose around a prominent lighthouse. Despite its official name, the natives call it **El Monumento de los Monos** *Bichis*, that is, the *Naked* Monkey Monument. From the indigenous Cahita language, **bichi** is readily understood in northwest Mexico. That's the bare truth.

CHAMARRA

FEELING a little chilly? Don't reach for your **chaqueta**, the standard word for *jacket*. Here it's a **chamarra**.

23

CHONES

Literal Meaning: undies

WITH so many working from home during the COVID-19 pandemic, looking well-dressed has only been important from the waist up. That led to:

Yo estaba en la reunión Zoom con mi corbata puesta y en mis **chones**.

I was in the Zoom meeting with my tie on and in my *underwear*.

Chones is the humorous abbreviation of **calzones**, plural of underwear.

 24

CUACHALOTE

IN the northwest, dress well, lest you be chided with this messy adjective:

Andas todo **cuachalote**. Cambia esos pantalones y métete bien la camisa.

You look *like a wreck*. Change those pants and tuck your shirt in well.

GONE WITH THE WIND

Like to chew the fat? In Mexico, choose the windy idiom **echar el chal**. Literally, it means to throw your shawl to the wind. In English, you will be shooting the breeze. Example: Pasé como media hora con Mariela, **echando el chal** nomás. Translation: I spent about a half an hour with Mariela, just *shooting the breeze*. Hopefully, your chat was like a breathe of fresh air.

 25

FACHOSO

Literal Meaning: face-like

FACCIA in modern Italian is the word for *face*. By extension, our face represents our entire appearance. This also appears as **andar en fachas**.

Me dio pena contestar la puerta porque andaba todo **fachoso**.

I was embarrassed to answer the door because I looked *like a mess*.

GANCHO

LITERAL MEANING: HOOK

NEED to hang up your clothes? Then ask for a **gancho**, not a **percha** as in many other Latin countries.

No seas malita. Préstame un **gancho** por favor.

Would you be so kind as to let me borrow a *clothes hanger*?

See also #359, **enganche**.

GUANGO

LITERAL MEANING: [UNKNOWN]

UNLESS you are after a hip-hop look, you will not be flattered to have your attire so described.

Cambíate esos pantalones. Están todos **guangos**.

Change those pants. They are *too baggy*.

IR COMO HILO DE MEDIA

LITERAL MEANING: TO LEAVE LIKE A SOCK THREAD

EVER decide to pull on that solitary string hanging from your sock? Careful! If not, it may completely unravel.

① Cuando en confianza, nos dejamos **ir como hilo de media** y lo contamos todo.
When we feel comfortable, we *let our hair down* and tell all.

It can also denote any situation that accelerates suddenly.

② En una semana, la canción **se fue como hilo de media** y ya cuenta con más de 74 millones de visitas en YouTube.

In just a week, the song's popularity *skyrocketed* and now boasts more than 74 million YouTube views.

LLEVAR DE CORBATA
LITERAL MEANING: TO TAKE BY THE TIE

THE tie hangs around our neck and must follow us, like it or not. Eating in haste? The poor tie gets stained with ketchup. Running to shred that confidential document? Watch out! Otherwise, the paper won't be the only victim. This sartorial idiom reaffirms that haste makes waste. It frequently appears in newspapers in highway casualty headlines.

Lo llevaron de corbata: pepenador atropellado en el kilómetro 45

Collateral damage: poor recycler run over at Kilometer 45

MEZCLILLAS
LITERAL MEANING: DENIMS

AMERICA has spread the blue jean craze the world over. Many Latin countries have adopted the English term *jeans*. But here preference goes to describing their fabric: denim.

Es momento de pánico; todas mis **mezclillas** están sucias.

It's panic time; all my *blue jeans* are dirty.

PLAYERA
LITERAL MEANING: THE BEACH THING

UNDER the intense Mexican sun, you will want to go to the beach as lightly clad as possible. If you choose to cover your upper torso, it will be with a **playera**, the local word for any T-shirt not considered underwear. For the latter, use **camiseta.**

En el tianguis compré cuatro **playeras** por 100 pesos.

At the outdoor street market, I picked up four *T-shirts* for 100 pesos.

EYES

A OJO DE BUEN CUBERO

LITERAL MEANING: TO THE EYE OF THE GOOD BUCKET MAKER

BEFORE the advent of plastics, vendors sold and dispensed liquids in small hand-made buckets. In Spanish the bucket is a **cubeta**, and the one who makes them, the **cubero**. How could he ensure that each bucket would be the same? He couldn't. He merely relied on his eyes. This phrase is your best bet to describe your best guess. Notice this comment in a product review:

> Lindísimo tapete, pero pensé que era más grande. Esto pasa por no medir y confiarse **a ojo de buen cubero**.

> Gorgeous rug, but I thought it was bigger. That's what happens for not measuring and just *eyeballing* it.

QUEDARSE CON EL OJO CUADRADO

LITERAL MEANING: TO END UP WITH A SQUARE EYE

WHAT effect do surprises have on you? Do you blush, cry or faint? In this geometric hyperbole, one's eyes become square.

> Cuando me duplicaron el sueldo, **me quedé con el ojo cuadrado**.

> When they doubled my salary, *I was beside myself*.

PARADO DE PESTAÑA

LITERAL MEANING: WITH STANDING EYELASHES

THEY say that the eyes are the windows to our soul. If that is so, then our eyelashes have a front seat to all the action. Does your friend have some especially exciting news for you? Then you might hear:

> Tenemos mucho que platicar; me tienes **parado de pestaña**.

> We have a lot to talk about; you have me *on the edge of my seat*.

TRAER ENTRE CEJA Y CEJA

LITERAL MEANING: TO BRING BETWEEN THE EYEBROWS

HOW is your intensity level? Body language experts report that when our eyebrows unite at a low middle position, it can indicate anger, frustration, or intense concentration. Its meaning will vary by context.

(1) **Traigo entre ceja y ceja** comprar un nuevo coche.
I have been mulling over buying a new car.

(2) Ese Ramón me **trae entre ceja y ceja**.
That Ramón *has a grudge against me.*

A headline on *El Financiero* posed the question:

(3) ¿Por qué tiene Estados Unidos **entre ceja y ceja** a Huawei?
Why is the US *fixated* on Huawei?

FEET

HAY QUE PONERSE EL HUARACHE ANTES DE ESPINARSE.

LITERAL MEANING: YOU HAVE TO PUT ON SANDALS BEFORE YOU GET PRICKED.

IN a country filled with cactuses, the last thing you want is to puncture your foot with a fallen needle. Solution? Just make sure you are wearing your **huaraches**, typical *leather sandals*. Need to offer a word of caution? Try this saying, which is a worthy equivalent of *An ounce of prevention is better than a pound of cure.*

THE EDIBLE SANDAL

Huaraches can help you avoid, not just the prick of cactus needles, but hunger pangs as well. How? Because it's also the designation for a tasty meal. These **huaraches** are fried, oblong corn-flour creations topped with meat, cheese and salsa. Go all out and pile on some sautéed **nopales**, real cactus ears— no needles included.

NO TE PONGAS CON SANSÓN A LAS PATADAS.

LITERAL MEANING: DON'T BECOME LIKE SAMPSON BEFORE THE KICKS.

BIBLICAL Sampson was unmatched in strength. If we perceive that our opponent is similarly endowed, we would do well to keep our distance. As structured, this saying means: *Go pick on someone your own size.* After an armored car crashed and destroyed a large public bus, one man tweeted:

Ahora sí el Metrobús **se puso con Sansón a las patadas**.

This time the Metrobus *picked on someone too big for him.*

HAIR

AGARRARSE DEL CHONGO

LITERAL MEANING: TO GRAB THE HAIR BUN

CAT FIGHT! That was the cry that rang out in school when two girls would skirmish. In Mexico, you are more likely to hear: **Se agarraron del chongo**. The **chongo** is the *hair bun*. But the phrase denotes a serious female battle, whether physical or verbal, hairstyle notwithstanding. More recently its usage encompasses any clash, regardless of sex. *El Sol de Sinaloa* reported:

Los diputados en tribuna **se agarraron del chongo** por un micrófono.

The congressmen in session *came to blows* over a microphone.

CUANDO LAS BARBAS DE TU VECINO VEAS AFEITAR, PON LAS TUYAS A REMOJAR.

LITERAL MEANING: WHEN YOU SEE YOUR NEIGHBOR'S BEARD CUT, SOAK YOURS.

BEFORE shaving cream's invention, a man would head to the barbershop to get his beard trimmed. Since facial hair can be especially resistant, the barber soaked the client's hair with a towel drenched in hot water. After a few minutes, the towel would come off, and the barber could easily trim away the softened hairs. An observant neighbor in need of a similar cut could facilitate the barber's work by pre-soaking his beard. Practical use? Pull out this saying when a crisis has arisen and people are not taking the necessary precautions, such as occurred during the Coronavirus pandemic as many brushed off wearing masks and social distancing. It's like saying: *See the writing on the wall and do something about it.*

HACER LA BARBA
LITERAL MEANING: TO DO THE BEARD

OH, the attentive barber! He took great pains to make you feel like a king when you were in his shop. "How do you want your sideburns? Should I take that stubble off your neck for you? How about I trim that beard?" It's not hard to see how doing the beard became an idiom for *buttering people up*.

No me hagas la barba. De todas formas no te voy a prestar nada.

Don't try to butter me up. Either way, I am not loaning you anything at all.

The sweet-talker himself is said to be a **barbero**.

MOVER EL BIGOTE
LITERAL MEANING: TO MOVE THE MUSTACHE

THE bold macho mustache is not as common as before. Nevertheless, that standard of male grooming persists in this hairy phrase.

Vamos, muchachos. Es hora de **mover el bigote**.

Let's go, guys. It's time *to eat*.

READY FOR GREEN HAIR?

Don't worry. You don't have to be a punk star; you just need to get mad.
In Mexican Spanish **sacar canas verdes**, literally *to grow green gray hairs*, takes anger to another level, or at least to another color. As an example: Mi hijo no me hace caso; me está **sacando canas verdes**. Translation: My son doesn't listen to me and he's *really getting on my nerves*.

HANDS

DAR ATOLE CON EL DEDO

LITERAL MEANING: TO GIVE A HOT CORN BEVERAGE WITH THE FINGER

IF there is anything that can grate on a parent's nerves, it is a baby's persistent cry, especially in the wee hours of the night. When hunger was at fault, mother had a trick up her sleeve. She would stick her finger into some **atole**, a hot corn-based beverage popular in Mexico, and give that smattering of food to the newborn. Of course, what the infant really wanted was mother's milk; mother was pulling a fast one. That's the idea behind this phrase. When one man's electric bill more than doubled during the pandemic, he protested to the electric company that had promised not to raise rates:

¡No más mentiras y **atole con el dedo**!

Stop lying and *pulling the wool over our eyes*!

ECHAR LA MANO

LITERAL MEANING: TO THROW THE HAND

NEED help? Do you really need a hand? Then, ask someone to throw it to you, Mexican style.

Échame la mano, manito.

Hey, bro, *give me a hand*.

MEXICAN TRASH TALK 101

Years ago, children would play with spinning tops and try to outdo one another. Imagine the skill required to get that top in sweet gyration, perfectly balanced on your fingernail—a true feat! Out of that childhood game came the in-your-face saying **Échate esa trompa a la uña**, literally, *throw that top on your fingernail*. Choose this saying when you want to rub your achievements in your opponent's face. It's the equivalent of: *Look who's laughing now!* Or perhaps: *How about them apples?* Remember, it's the way to let your opponent know that you nailed it.

HEALTH

---

 1 44

CHIPOTE

FROM the Nahuatl *xixipóchtic*, a **chipote** is the lump that forms when you get hit on the head. By extension, you might see:

① ¿Cómo puede reparar los **chipotes** en sus llantas?
How can you repair the *bulges* on your tires?

② Dos semanas después de la fiesta, vimos un **chipote** en la curva del virus.
Two weeks after the party, we saw a *bump* in the virus's curve.

 1 45

CHOCHOS

LITERAL MEANING: [IN THE ANDES] A KIND OF BEANS

EVER visited a homeopathic doctor? In many countries they dispense medicine in the form of little white balls, known here as **chochos**. This has given rise to the verb **chochear**, *to convalesce*, and to the noun **chochero**, the *homeopathic doctor* himself.

Ya tiene 90 años. Se la pasa **chocheando**.

He's already 90 years old. He just spends his time *taking pills*.

 1 46

CUERPO CORTADO

LITERAL MEANING: CUT BODY

FROM the sound of it, you might think that this term would describe the effects of a serious automobile accident. Here, though, it's merely a graphic description of flu symptoms.

Tengo fiebre y **cuerpo cortado**.

I've got a fever and *body aches*.

1 47

GRIPA

IN most Latin countries, you can come down with a case of **gripe**, that is, the flu. But locally it takes a female form: **gripa**.

¿Tiene la **gripa**? Vete con el chochero.

Do you have the *flu*? Go see the homeopathic doctor.

 1 48

MORMADO
LITERAL MEANING: HAVING GLANDERS (A DISEASE THAT MAINLY AFFECTS HORSES)

ALTHOUGH glanders, or **muermo** in Spanish, is a disease that principally affects horses and other animals, one of its symptoms, states the *Merck Veterinary Manual*, is "high fever… and a thick, nasal discharge." It is easy to imagine how some jokester began to apply the term to humans. If you have the flu, you might describe your symptoms as:

Doctor, tengo un fiebre alto y estoy **mormado**.

Doctor, I have a high fever and I'm *all stuffed up*.

 1 49

REGADERA
LITERAL MEANING: THE WATERING THING

NEED a shower? If so, you won't take a **ducha**, as in many Latin countries, but rather head to the **regadera**, the *shower*. One man tweeted:

① Ya estoy enfadado de bañarme en mi **regadera** y no en la playa.
I am sick of bathing in my *shower* and not at the beach.

A Mexican might also announce:

② Me voy a **dar un regaderazo**.
I'm going *to take a shower*.

LEGS

CHAMORRO

LITERAL MEANING: SHAVED ANIMAL HEAD

MEET the local word for the *calf*, that fleshy back part of your leg below the knee. This differs from the standard Spanish **pantorilla**. Once again the word started with animals and migrated to humans. Sound familiar?

Híjole, me duele el **chamorro** después de tanto ejercicio.

Man, my *calf* really hurts after so much exercise.

MOUTH

ANDAR CON EL JESÚS EN LA BOCA

LITERAL MEANING: TO WALK WITH THE JESUS IN THE MOUTH

IT'S almost midnight and your son was supposed to be home from the party two hours ago! How do you feel? Anguished? That's an understatement. If minutes later the young man finally appears, a Mexican mother might well chastise him with:

Hijo, ¿dónde estuviste? Desde hace horas, ¡he **andado con el Jesús en la boca**!

Son, where have you been? For hours I *have been worried sick about you*!

CHIMUELO

LITERAL MEANING: MOLARS

MISSING a few teeth? In that case, here you will be described as **chimuelo**, or *toothless*. The movie *How to Train Your Dragon* features a fire-breather named Toothless. In the Spanish dubbing for Latin America he became **Chimuelo**. Moral of the story? Just keep flossing.

Aquí el más **chimuelo** masca fierro.

Here even the most *toothless* of men chews iron. [*Even our weaklings are tough.*]

1 53

HASTA POR DEBAJO DE LA LENGUA
LITERAL MEANING: EVEN UNDER THE TONGUE

HOW thoroughly did your team beat its opponent? Were they crushed, demolished or blown out? Why not try this sublingual equivalent?

① Ganaron 10-0. Les dieron **hasta por debajo de la lengua**.
They won 10-0. They *obliterated* them.

② En el aeropuerto lo revisaron **hasta por debajo de la lengua**.
At the airport they inspected *every inch of his body*.

NOSE
---

1 54

¡FÚCHILA!

WHAT is that horrible stench? Are your olfactory senses in protest? Or are you upset about a bad situation? Then blare out this interjection of disgust.

① **¡Fúchila!** Hueles a humo.   ② Jaqueca, aléjate. **¡Fúchila!**
Gross! You smell like smoke.   Migraine, get lost. *How horrible!*

SKIN
---

1 55

GÜERO

THEY say that blondes have more fun. While that's debatable, it's a sure thing that your golden hair will result in Mexicans applying this adjective to you. On the other hand, when you visit the market, sellers will call you **güero** to butter you up and spur sales, regardless of your skin and hair color. Note that such color references are not prejudicial, but rather terms of endearment.

① Roberto está noviando con la **güerita** de al lado.
Roberto is dating the *blonde girl* next door.

② Pásele, **güerito**, ¿qué le ofrecemos?
Como on in, *buddy*, what are you looking for?

71

ENCHINARSE LA PIEL

LITERAL MEANING: TO MAKE YOUR SKIN CHINESE

EVER witnessed a performance so exceptional that it gave you goosebumps? In said circumstances, Mexicans would say that their skin gets "Chinese." Despite this, the reference has no relation to Asians of any kind. Rather, during the Spanish conquest, the invaders imposed a racial caste system. The descendants of a black and Spaniard would be considered **mulatos**. If a **mulato** married a Spanish woman and had children, these offspring were considered **moriscos**. If a **morisco** paired with a Spaniard, their child would be **chino**. This gene pool frequently produced wavy hair; hence, to this day in Mexico **pelo chino** is *wavy hair*. It would appear that those same waves transferred to the skin in this idiom.

Cuando la escuché cantar, **se me enchinó la piel**.

When I heard her sing, *it gave me goosebumps*.

ALL THINGS CHINESE

If you don't understand something, just protest: **Está en chino**. Literally, that means: *It's in Chinese*. Mexicans will call anyone with Asian features **chino**, even if they are Korean or Japanese. Don't be offended. They will also dub all whites **gringos**, even if they're not Americans. Asian eyes are described as **ojos rasgados**, literally *scratched eyes*, since they appear that way from a distance. We, though, are left merely scratching our heads.

UPPER TORSO

A PAPUCHI

FOR some, one of the fondest childhood memories is that of your father or mother carrying you piggyback. In Northwestern Mexico use this option, sometimes written **a capuchi**. In standard Spanish it is **de caballito**. This term varies greatly by region, so ask around for the local equivalent.

Papí, llévame **a papuchi** hasta el mar.

Daddy, carry me *piggyback* down to the ocean.

PONERSE DE PECHITO

LITERAL MEANING: TO PUT ONESELF ON THE SIDE OF THE CHEST

HAVE you ever gotten yourself in trouble by sticking your nose where it didn't belong? Or maybe sticking your neck out for someone? In this example, similar misfortune may befall you if you stick out your chest.

① Creo en darles segundas oportunidades a la personas.
   Pero no hay por qué **ponerse de pechito**.
   I believe in giving people second chances. But there is no reason
   to put yourself in harm's way.

② Si sabes que la pandemia es seria, ¿porque **te pones de pechito**?
   If you know how serious the pandemic is, why are you *risking it*?

WAIST

CON LA MANO
EN LA CINTURA

LITERAL MEANING: WITH YOUR HAND ON THE WAIST

AS a child, when you finally mastered riding a bike, you may have exclaimed: "Look, Mom. No hands!". Or a guru in any field might boast: "I can do it with my eyes closed." In Mexico, just put your hand on your waist.

A: ¿Crees que Roberto pueda diseñar una app
   para nosotros?

B: **¡Con la mano en la cintura!**

A: Do you think Roberto can design an app for us?

B: He can do it *in his sleep*!

LONJA

Literal Meaning: a long, wide cut of meat

WATCHING one's waist may only lead to disappointment, because for many of us, it has grown larger than expected.

Espero que la sauna me ayude a bajar esa **lonja**.

I hope the sauna helps me get rid of this *spare tire* [around my waist].

MINGITORIO

Literal Meaning: peeing place

THROUGHOUT most of Latin America, if you go into a public men's room, a man will urinate in a **urinal**. But not in Mexico; here's it's a **mingitorio**. One man tweeted:

Recuerda que el celular cuenta con 30 veces más microbios que el **mingitorio**.

Remember that a cell phone has 30 times more microbes than a *urinal*.

SIGNS OF THE TIMES

One of the first things a foreigner learns to say is: **¿Dónde está el baño?** (Where is the bathroom?) Of course, asking the question is just the beginning of the odyssey. If you are looking for a sign that announces **BAÑO**, you may find yourself going in circles. Instead, in many places you will encounter: **WC**. That's not Winston Churchill, but **water closet**. It is baffling that a term now seldom heard in English could be the standard sign in a foreign language.

The Bright Side

AFFIRMATION

¡ÁNDALE, PUES!

LITERAL MEANING: WALK TO IT, THEN!

READY to agree to a proposal? Reply with this.

① A: Nos vemos a las cuatro.   A: We'll see you at four.
    B: ¡Ándale, pues!   B: *Sounds good.*

Conversely, push others to get things done with ¡**Ándale**!

② Vete a hacer tus tareas. ¡**Ándale**!
    Go do your homework. *Get to it!*

¡ÉCOLE!

LITERAL MEANING: HERE THEY ARE [ITALIAN: ECCOLE QUA]

CONSIDER this Italian import as another way to say: **Así es**, or *That's right*.

A: ¿Estos limones están en oferta?   A: These lemons are on sale?

B: ¡**École**! Están a mitad de precio.   B: *That's right!* They're half off.

¡FIERRO, PARIENTE!

LITERAL MEANING: IRON, RELATIVE!

IN northern Mexico and especially in Sonora, you will hear this phrase regularly. The **fierro**, or iron, refers to a firearm, but as a unit it indicates agreement and wholehearted support. Its meaning ranges from *Right on!* to *Let's do it!* or *Go for it!*.

A: ¿Vamos a la fiesta mañana?   A: Are we going to the party tomorrow?

B: ¡**Fierro, pariente**!   B: *Let's do it, bro.*

Other variants include: ¡**Fierro, machuca**! and ¡**Fierro a las 300**!—all with similar meanings.

¿SALE?

LITERAL MEANING: LEAVE?

SINCE **salir** in Spanish means *to leave*, you might think at first that the speaker is suggesting that you hit the road, but all to the contrary. He's merely asking you for the green light. If you are in accord, respond with another **Sale**. If you are really in accord, or just want to rhyme, opt for **Sale vale**.

A: Te pago mañana a las 8. ¿**Sale**?

B: Sale vale.

A: I'll pay you tomorrow at 8. *OK?*

B: Okie dokey.

¡YA MERITO!

LITERAL MEANING: THE VERY NOW!

AS a child, long road trips seemed eternal. When would we arrive? "We're almost there" our parents chimed. Select this local equivalent for the same. Exhausted of unending COVID-19 isolation precautions, one woman posted:

Me siento como el burro de Shrek preguntando, ¿**Ya merito**?.

I feel like Shrek's donkey always asking: *Are we there yet?*.

BEAUTY

A TODO DAR

LITERAL MEANING: AT ALL GIVING

THERE's more happiness in giving than receiving, as this generous idiom suggests. Its meaning varies greatly by context. Note these tweets:

① Mi bici ya está bien viejita, pero me ha dejado rodar **a todo dar**.
My bike is really old, but it has allowed me to have a *beautiful* ride.

② Mi hermana debe tener locos a los vecinos cantando **a todo dar**.
My sister must be driving the neighbors nuts singing *at the top of her lungs*.

③ ¡Que se lo pases **a todo dar**!
Have a *great* time!

CHULO

LITERAL MEANING: PRETTY

EMBRACE this popular synonym for **bonito**—*pretty* or *beautiful*. Ever visit San Diego, California? Then perhaps you've heard of the suburb known as Chula Vista. This literally means *Beautiful View*. The noun form is **chulada**, popular in the exclamation: ¡**Qué chulada**!

① ¡Qué **chula** la playera!
What a *beautiful* T-shirt!

② ¡Qué **chulada** de mujer!
What a *beautiful* woman!

¡QUÉ CHIDO!

ESPECIALLY popular around Mexico City, **chido** also describes the beautiful and the cool.

¡**Qué chido** el coche nuevo de tu abuela!

Your grandma's new car is *really cool!*

In northern Mexico, change the *d* for an *l*. ¡**Qué chilo**!

¡QUÉ CURADA!

LITERAL MEANING: How cured!

IN Mexico's far northwest corner sits the city of Tijuana, on the border with Southern California. This is their regional equivalent of ¡**Qué chido**! above. One man posted this:

¡**Qué curado** estaría escaparnos e irnos a la playa!

How *great* it would be to get away and go to the beach!

Conversely, in Monterrey and Guadalajara, it takes on the sense of *comical*.

¡**Qué curada** esa película!

What a *funny* movie!

¡QUÉ PADRE!

LITERAL MEANING: HOW PRIEST!

IMAGINE the scene: You come from a good Catholic family and your dad just bought a new car. But before driving it around town, tradition dictated that he have it blessed by the local priest, known in Spanish as the **padre**. The same was expected for any valuable item, even property. Thus a connection grew between shiny, new possessions and the priest. When San Diego was awarded a Major League baseball team, what did they call it? The **Padres**! Few fans realize that the name of the team in plain English is the San Diego *Priests*. This also explains why in other parts of the country the synonym ¡**Qué curada**! is popular. **Cura** is merely another term for *priest*.

①   ¡**Qué padre** que regresen los autocinemas!
     It's *so cool* that the drive-in theaters are back!

②   ¡Esa chamarra está **padrísima**!
     That sweater is *so beautiful!*

COMEDY

COTORREAR

LITERAL MEANING: TO TALK TOO MUCH

Add this verb to your vocabulary to describe casual chatting or mere joking.

①   El confinamiento me tiene tan aburrido que ayer me marcó un extorsionador y acabamos **cotorreando**.
     I was so bored in confinement that yesterday a con artist called and we ended up *chatting*.

②   No te precoupes. Solo te estaba **cotorreando**.
     Don't worry. I was just *kidding*.

1 73

ECHAR CARRILLA

LITERAL MEANING: TO THROW THE LITTLE FACE

ENJOY joking around and teasing your friends? If so, this idiom is for you.

① Toda la tarde se la pasaron **echando carrilla**.
They spent the whole afternoon *joking around*.

② Lo bueno es que sé aguantar la **carrilla**, aunque en ocasiones duele.
It's good that I can handle all the *teasing*, even though sometimes it hurts.

1 74

AHHHHH [FAKE LAUGH]

I call this the fake laugh, not because of insincerity, but because it is a deliberate laugh that Mexicans insert into conversations as if to say, "I'm just joking." It is nasal, drawn out a couple of seconds, and sounds like the buzzer that goes off on game shows when someone gives the wrong answer.

Después de todo esto, no voy a quitar mi tapabocas, ni cuando beso a mi novia. **Ahhhhh**. No te creas.

After all of this, I'm not going to take my mask off, not even when I kiss my girlfriend. [*Buzzer sound*] Just kidding!

ENCOURAGEMENT
---

 1 75

APAPACHAR

LITERAL MEANING: TO SQUEEZE

NEED a hug? Who doesn't? The Aztecs embraced the idea in Nahuatl with the verb *patzoa*, to squeeze. Today **apapachar** is not limited to hugging; rather, it encompasses showing affection in any number of ways.

① Voy a comprarle a mi mamá su comida favorita para **apapacharla**.
I am going to buy Mom her favorite food *to treat her*.

② Esposa a esposo: Hoy necesito que me **apapaches**.
Wife to husband: Today I need some *TLC*.

ECHAR FLORES

LITERAL MEANING: TO THROW FLOWERS

NOTHING smells more fragrant than compliments thrown your way. Those are the figurative flowers in this botanical metaphor.

No te estoy **echando flores**. De verdad cantas muy bonito.

I am not trying *to flatter* you. You really do sing beautifully.

ECHARLE GANAS

LITERAL MEANING: TO THROW TO HIM THE DESIRE

ARE you discouraged, recovering from an illness or financial setback? In these circumstances Mexicans will aim to comfort you, no matter your plague, with this phrase. While the intentions are good, for those who suffer it comes across as empty advice. You might think: "I am already doing all I can. My problems are not due to a lack of effort."

A: Estoy muy enfermo.

A: I am very sick.

B: Pos, **échate ganas** y te vas a recuperar.

B: Well, *do all you can* to get better.

¡ÓRALE!

LITERAL MEANING: NOW TO IT!

IN Spanish **ahora** means *now*. Locally, it was cut to **ora** and **le** was added for emphasis. This multipurpose interjection is quintessentially Mexican.

① ¡**Órale**, te estás tardando!
   Hurry up! You're taking too long!

② Vete a hacer tus tareas. ¡**Órale**!
   Go do your homework. *Get to it!*

③ ¡**Órale**! Te presto el dinero.
   OK, I'll loan you the money.

OPPORTUNISM

HACER LEÑA DEL ÁRBOL CAÍDO

LITERAL MEANING: TO MAKE FIREWOOD FROM THE FALLEN TREE

WHEN life gives you lemons, you make lemonade. And when the storm knocks down a tree or two, don't worry; enjoy the free firewood.

> No es que quiera **hacer leña del árbol caído**, pero como Edgar ya se fue, ¿podría yo ocupar su oficina?
>
> It's not that I am trying *to take advantage of the situation*, but since Edgar left, could I move in to his office?

PUENTE

LITERAL MEANING: BRIDGE

IF Point A and Point B are separated by a chasm, a bridge will make your journey shorter. However, in this type of bridge, it lengthens it—in a good way. Locally, it means a *long weekend*.

> ¡Qué padre! ¡Este fin de semana hay **puente**!
>
> Awesome! This is a *long weekend*!

SUCCESS

LIBRARLO

LITERAL MEANING: TO FREE IT

EVER been suddenly freed of punishment or perhaps a disaster? If so, you'll get the gist of the way this verb is used here.

(1) Pensé que iba a reprobar la matemática, pero **lo libré**.
   I thought I was going to flunk math, but somehow I *made it*.

(2) El policía me iba a multar, pero al final **lo libré**.
   The policeman was going to fine me, but in the end *I got away with it*.

The Dark Side

CORRUPTION

CHAPUCERO

LITERAL MEANING: A POOR-QUALITY WORKER

IN standard Spanish **chapucero** is an adjective describing a botched job. When a project fails to meet the customer's expectation, he feels cheated. That's the extended meaning here.

> Ese Carlos siempre gana en póker. Es **chapucero**.

> That Carlos always wins at poker. He's a *cheater*.

CHUECO

LITERAL MEANING: BOW-LEGGED

IF you have been taught to walk the straight and narrow, **chueco** is just the opposite. It refers to what is crooked, in any sense.

① Dame otro clavo. Este está **chueco**.
Give me another nail. This one is *crooked*.

② No confío en ese doctor. Es **chueco**.
I don't trust that doctor. He's *dishonest*.

EL GANDALLA NO BATALLA.

LITERAL MEANING: THE ONE WHO GOES AHEAD DOESN'T BATTLE.

THE light is red and you are hopelessly stuck in traffic. Suddenly, however, a bus jumps onto the shoulder of the highway, passes all traffic and then, given the opportunity, scuttles through the still-red light. Enter the **gandalla**, the selfish opportunist for whom law and order are mere suggestion. One man confronted the phone company, complaining:

> ¡Hoy se pasaron de **gandalla**! ¡Dos facturas en un solo mes!

> Today you took *jerk* to a new level! Two bills in one month!

Our best translation for the above saying? *The jerk doesn't work.*

EL QUE NO TRANZA, NO AVANZA.

LITERAL MEANING: HE WHO DOESN'T CHEAT, DOESN'T MOVE FORWARD.

WHO says that honesty is the best policy? Apparently few today, as evidenced by this popular saying. Here **tranzar** means *to cheat*. At least one young man seems to buck the trend. He posted:

Prefiero morir pobre que ser **tranza**.

I prefer to be poor than a *cheat*.

LA CHOTA

POSSIBLY an import of the English verb *shutter*, **chota** is a slang term for the police. The *Diccionario del español de México* offers this example:

① ¡Aguas, ahí viene **la chota**!

Look out! The *cops* are coming!

If an individual policeman is the subject, use the masculine definite article.

② **El chota** me paró.

The *cop* stopped me.

TAKING A BITE OUT OF CRIME?

If you have the displeasure of being stopped by a policeman, instead of taking a bite out of crime, he will likely try to take a bite out of you! How so? He may ask for a **mordida**, literally a *bite*. What he's really fishing for is a bribe.

RATERO

LITERAL MEANING: THE RAT GUY

RODENTS are disgusting. Ditto for thieves.

No entres en ese fraccionamiento. Son puros **rateros**.

Don't go into that neighborhood. They're a bunch of *thieves*.

DEATH
---

 1 88

CHUPAR FAROS
LITERAL MEANING: TO SUCK LIGHTHOUSES

YOU have been condemned to death and will be executed within hours. What will you request as a last wish? According to one theory, during the Mexican Revolution, some poor souls asked for a smoke. What brand? One of the cheapest available: **Faros**. The prisoner would take a few puffs and then be led off to the firing squad. His last wish became a euphemism for death.

① A: ¿Qué se hizo el ratero de abajo?   A: Where did that thief downstairs go?
   B: Ya **chupó faros**.   B: He *kicked the bucket.*

② A: ¿Qué pasó con la licuadora?   A: What happened to the blender?
   B: Ya **chupó faros**.   B: It *bit the dust.*

 1 89

PETATEAR
LITERAL MEANING: TO RUG

BACK in the Aztecs' heyday, when someone in the family died, their cadaver was rolled up in a **petate**, a kind of natural-fiber rug or mat, and was buried. Since the **petate** was also a makeshift bed, it is fitting that the deceased would sleep on in death itself—and in their own bed. One woman tweeted:

Tengo ganas de limpiar con mucho cloro…de esas limpiadas que casi
me petateo con el olor.

I feel like cleaning with a lot of bleach…one of those cleanings where the smell
almost makes me *keel over.*

THE FLEETING RUG BURN

The **petate** has survived in other figures of speech as well. Ever been excited—ecstatic—about some news only to have your hopes dashed? Then the joy you experienced was a mere **llamarada de petate**, or rug flame. Since the natural fibers of this organic mat were highly combustible, they could be used as kindling.
Of course, the flame they produced was short-lived. If you experience this kind of rug burn, your happiness is just a *flash in the pan.*

DECEIT

BAILÁRSELO

LITERAL MEANING: TO BE DANCED UPON

BUY your house for a song and a dance? Then it was a bargain! You barely broke a sweat. On the other hand, according to this colorful verb, if you get danced on, you have been swindled.

① Llegas emocionado a comer lo guardado, y al darte cuenta, **te lo bailaron**.
You arrive excited to eat what you saved, only to realize you've been *duped*.

② **Se lo bailaron** con un billete falso.
They *scammed* him with a counterfeit bill.

CAER REDONDO

LITERAL MEANING: TO FALL ROUND

THE laws of physics dictate that if two objects of different weights are dropped simultaneously from the third floor to the sidewalk below, they will fall at the same speed. At least that's true in a vacuum. In the real world, if you take a one-pound weight and tie it to a kite and then drop it from the third story, its descent will not be as fast. We've altered the aerodynamics. Physics aside, in Mexican Spanish when you fall *round*, you have either taken a serious tumble or have been completely fooled. You fell for it 100%.

① Al volver a casa, me resbalé y **caí redondo**.
Coming home, I slipped and *fell flat on my face*.

② Llegué tan cansado que **caí redondo** en la cama.
I came home so tired that I *collapsed* onto the bed.

③ Le vendieron el coche a doble el precio y **cayó redondo**.
They sold him the car for double the price and *he fell for it*.

1 92

CARRANCEAR
LITERAL MEANING: TO ACT LIKE CARRANZA

VENUSTIANO Carranza served as Mexico's 37th president from 1917 to 1920. Rampant corruption during his term spawned a new verb.

A: ¿Qué pasó con el proyector?

B: Los jefes lo **carrancearon**.

A: What happened to the projector?

B: The bosses *swiped* it.

1 93

CHAMAQUEARLE
LITERAL MEANING: TO BOY HIM

BOYS will be boys. And mischief follows.

Nos **chamaquearon** con el Tratado de Libre Comercio.

We got *suckered* with the Free Trade Agreement.

1 94

CHOREAR

DON'T confuse this verb with **chorrear**, which means *to pour*. With one *r*, what is being poured are persuasive, manipulating, and deceitful words.

¡No me vayas a **chorear**!

Don't try to *sweet-talk* me!

1 95

NO ME VENGAS CON QUE A CHUCHITA LA BOLSEARON.
LITERAL MEANING: DON'T COME TO ME WITH [THE STORY] THAT LITTLE JESUSA WAS PICKPOCKETED.

URBAN legend has it that hundreds of years ago a certain Jesusa, nicknamed Chuchita, labored as a maid. When her employers sent her to buy groceries, she would come back empty-handed. Her justification? **Me bolsearon,** that is, a pick-pocket must have taken it. Much like the boy who cried wolf, Chuchita's excuse soon became worn-out. If your child or someone under your supervision makes a habit of rationalizing his failures, just counter with this saying. It means: *Don't come to me with the same lame excuses!*

DISCIPLINE

DAR UN CHICOTAZO
LITERAL MEANING: TO GIVE A WHIPPING

HEAVYWEIGHT champion Mohammed Ali once boasted: "I fly like a butterfly, I sting like a bee." In contrast, in the Aztec world a featherweight was a particular menace; the *xicotl* wasp also knew a thing or two about stinging. From this word, the Mexican Spanish **chicote** was born, initially an *animal whip*. It now encompasses any physical or figurative whipping. One post read:

(1)   ¡Corre, que tu papá te va a **dar un chicotazo**!
      Run, your dad is going to give you a *whipping*!

News portal *ADN Informativo* had the following headline:

(2)   Después de un choque, toma en cuenta el **chicotazo** para prevenir
      futuras lesiones

      After an accident, take into account *whiplash* to prevent future injuries

LEERLE LA CARTILLA
LITERAL MEANING: TO READ THE MANUAL TO SOMEONE

Outstanding vocalists can sing the telephone directory. But who wants a superior to read them a boring manual? That's the premise of this phrase.

Cuando José comenzó a faltar al trabajo, el jefe **le leyó la cartilla**.

When José started to miss work, the boss *read him the riot act*.

FAILURE

 1 98

AHOGADO EL NIÑO, TAPADO EL POZO.
LITERAL MEANING: DROWNED CHILD, COVERED WELL.

WHEN will you get the brakes fixed on your car? After you have an accident? When will you wear a mask and distance yourself? After you've been infected? This saying suggests that sometimes measures are not taken until after a problem has arisen. English translation? *Too little, too late.*

1 99

CARGARLE EL PAYASO
LITERAL MEANING: THE CLOWN CARRIES SOMEONE

ADRENALINE rushes through your veins as you head into the rodeo to face the bull. He rushes towards you. You lunge at the last second to avoid him, but he veers towards you and gashes your leg. There you lie injured and bleeding, and the bull is heading back your way. How will you escape? Unlikely heroes descend onto the field dressed as clowns, or **payasos**. One or more distract the bull, while another scoops you up and carries you to safety. In Mexican Spanish, then, if the clown carries you, you are in serious trouble. From the Twitterverse:

> Es necesario proteger a nuestros doctores. Si ellos caen, ¡**ya nos cargó el payaso**!

> We need to protect our doctors If they fall, *we are all fried*!

 2 00

DARSE UN RANAZO
LITERAL MEANING: TO HAVE A FROG SLAP

IT's raining and the city bus has just plastered a poor frog onto the highway. To say that the frog is dead is an understatement. He has been disemboweled and flattened like a flour tortilla. Select this phrase to describe a hard fall.

> Ayer me resbalé y **me di un ranazo**.

> Yesterday I slipped and *fell and hurt myself.*

2 01

DARLE EN LA TORRE

LITERAL MEANING: TO HIT SOMEONE IN THE TOWER

IN chess, the rook (Spanish: **torre**) is a valuable piece. If your opponent removes it, you are in dire straits. Similarly, if our body were a building, the tower would be our head, again a vital part of our organism. Choose this strategic idiom when you have been hit where it hurts.

Soy electricista y no puedo hacer trabajo desde la casa; **me dieron en la torre**.

I'm an electrician and I can't work from home; *this hits me where it hurts*.

2 02

LLOVER EN LA MILPITA

LITERAL MEANING: TO RAIN IN THE LITTLE CORN FIELD

RAIN is a double-edged sword: too much provokes flooding and not enough shrivels crops. Maybe that's why this phrase announces either a boon or a bane, depending on context. Option 1 is from *El Siglo de Torreón*:

① La depreciación del peso frente al dólar se resentirá en el bolsillo en los próximos meses…no nos deja de **llover en la milpita**.
The peso's depreciation against the dollar will be felt in our pockets in the coming months…*it's one problem after another*.

② ¡Qué audífonos más fifís! Parece que ya **llovió en la milpita**.
What fancy headphones! Looks like *someone struck it rich*.

See also #214, **llover sobremojado**.

2 03

REGARLA

LITERAL MEANING: TO WATER IT

WOULD you water down the truth? That would be a big mistake. This curious verb, always with the pronoun **la**, signals a greater blunder.

Está a punto de **regarla**.

He's about to *screw up*.

TOCARLE BAILAR CON LA MÁS FEA

LITERAL MEANING: TO BE YOUR TURN TO DANCE WITH THE UGLIEST GIRL

YOU have been at the dance for more than a few minutes, and all the guests have sized up the field of potential partners. Not able to muster the courage to ask a beautiful girl to the floor, you procrastinate—a seismic miscalculation. As the next song begins, you scan the field. To your chagrin there is but one candidate left: the ugliest girl of all. Yikes! Summon this woeful metaphor the next time calamity befalls you. An older gentleman posted:

> Hoy hace un año que me casé y bailé con la más guapa. Diez días después vino el derrame y **me tocó bailar con la más fea**.
>
> Today one year ago I got married and danced with the most beautiful woman. Ten days later I had a stroke and had to dance with *Murphy's Law*.

In other contexts it may translate to: *I drew the short straw*.

FIGHT

BRONCA

LITERAL MEANING: UNTAMED

IN English a bronco is a wild horse. Would you be willing to break one in? That's a hazardous task, not for the faint of heart. The same goes for fights and other problems.

① Se armó una **bronca** entre los pandilleros.
A *fight* broke out between gang members.

② Temo que mi sentido de humor un día me vaya a meter en una **bronca**.
I fear that my sense of humor one day is going to get me in *trouble*.

FANCY SOME UNTAMED MILK?

If your travels take you to rural Mexico, you may be offered some **leche bronca**. What, pray tell, is untamed milk? It refers to *unpasteurized* milk; it hasn't been tamed of the bacteria yet. See also term #255, **pajarete**.

---

2 06

MITOTE

FROM the Nahuatl *mitotique*, a indigenous dancer at a party where liquor ran freely, **mitote** today is a reference either to wild parties or bedlam.

① Extraño salir al **mitote**.

I miss the *wild parties*.

② Después de la violencia racial, se armó el **mitote**.

After the racial violence, *all pandemonium* broke loose.

IRRITATIONS

2 07

CAER GORDO

LITERAL MEANING: TO FALL FAT

IN this case you don't fall *flat* on your face, your fall *fat* on your face. Obesity has long been out of style in this chunky idiom, which means to hate or greatly dislike.

① Como **me cae gordo** que se vaya el Internet a cada rato.

How *I hate it* when the Internet goes out all the time.

② ¿Hay alguien en el trabajo que **le caiga gordo**?

Is there anyone at work *that you can't stand*?

2 08

LEPERADAS

FOUR-letter words are just part of **leperada**'s family. It encompasses any vulgar words or speech. The adjectival form is **lépero**.

① Cuando le reclamaron sus ausencias, respondió con puras **leperadas**.

Faced with complaints of his absences, he replied with nothing but *vulgarities*.

② No seas **lépero** ni inculto.

Be neither *foul-mouthed* nor unmannered.

PASARSE DE TUESTE

LITERAL MEANING: TO GO OVERBOARD ON THE TOASTING

PROCESSING coffee requires finesse and precision. Too much time in the sun and the light roast becomes a medium roast. If it's already a dark roast, then the extra exposure will ruin it. Consider this coffee comparison when a friend has been sunburned or has otherwise gone too far.

① ¿Estás bien, no tienes fiebre? ¿Ya te checaste o **te pasaste de tueste**?
Are you OK? You don't have a fever? Did you get checked or *is it too late*?

② Parece que **te pasaste de tueste**.
Looks like *you got a little too much sun.*

PELARLE

LITERAL MEANING: TO PEEL SOMEONE

WOULD it be easy to peel a potato while distracted? Of course not! You have to keep your eyes peeled; you must concentrate. In our lives we would like for our friends and family to have the same consideration when we speak.

① Siempre quien sí me interesa no **me pela**.
It always happens that the one I'm interested in doesn't even *know I exist.*

② Esposa al marido: No **me pelas**.
Wife to husband: You never *show me any attention.*

PLAGUES

CALLE DE LA AMARGURA

LITERAL MEANING: BITTERNESS STREET

HAVING a hard time of it? Financial setbacks? Loss of loved ones? Then welcome to One Bitterness Street, Home of the Wretched.

Los exámenes me traen por la **calle de la amargura**.
Exams have made *my life miserable.*

2 12

CAERLE EL CHAHUISTLE

LITERAL MEANING: TO HAVE THE CORN PLAGUE FALL ON SOMEONE

IF there were a Hall of Fame for crops, Mexicans would unanimously elect corn on the first vote. Without it, where would a family get the prime material for tortillas, tamales, and so many other corn creations? It's no wonder that **chahuistle**, a plague that affected corn and other grains, was a feared enemy.

Hoy perdí mi empleo. Ahora sí **nos cayó el chahuistle**.

Today I lost my job. Now *we're really in trouble*.

2 13

HACÉRSELE
LA VIDA DE CUADRITOS

LITERAL MEANING: YOUR LIFE BECOMES LITTLE SQUARES.

TAKE a precious vase and smash it onto the concrete floor. The result? It will be smashed to pieces. It is unlikely that those pieces will be square. In either case, if you are squaring off with someone who is making your life impossible, this idiom may check your box, as is evidenced by the following tweet:

Neta que yo no entiendo porque cuando se separan siempre le andan queriendo **hacer la vida de cuadritos** al ex.

The truth is I don't understand why in a separation they go around trying *to make* the ex's *life a living hell*.

2 14

LLOVER SOBREMOJADO

LITERAL MEANING: TO RAIN ON TOP OF WHAT'S WET

THE ground is drenched, completely saturated, and yet it keeps raining. Will it do any good? Of course, not. It's overkill.

Primero llegó la pandemia y luego el huracán. Está **lloviendo sobremojado**.

First came the pandemic and then the hurricane. *When it rains, it pours*.

METERSE EN CAMISA DE ONCE VARAS

LITERAL MEANING: TO PUT ON AN ELEVEN-ROD SHIRT

THINKING about adopting a child? In the Middle Ages in the adoption ceremony, the new father would put an over-size shirt over the head of his new son or daughter. He would then pull the child out the neck of the shirt and kiss him on the forehead. It was official! They were father and son! That was no small responsibility; over time, it could lead to serious problems.

> Poco después de iniciar la renovación de la casa, me di cuenta que **me había metido en camisa de once varas**.

> Shortly after starting to remodel my home, I realized that *I had opened a can of worms*.

SCHOOL

ACORDEÓN

LITERAL MEANING: ACCORDION

DIDN'T study for that final exam? For the dishonest, that was no sweat. They pulled a neatly folded paper out of their pocket, a cheat sheet.

> Cuando sacas el **acordeón** a mitad del examen y el profe se te queda viendo, ya sabes que estás en problemas.

> When you pull out the *cheat sheet* halfway through the exam and the teacher is staring at you, you know you're in trouble.

IRSE DE PINTA

LITERAL MEANING: TO GO PAINTED

IF you went out to paint the town red when you should have been in class, you will identify with this phrase.

> Fui mal alumno. Solía **irme de pinta**.

> I was a bad student. I used to *play hookie*.

6

All in the Family

ADULTS

AMÁ Y APÁ

Literal Meaning: [M]om and [D]ad

WHAT'S missing here? The initial letters, of course. We expect such babblings from the mouths of infants; they may be among their first words. What you may not expect, however, is that adult children perpetuate this kindergarten-esque shortcut throughout life as a term of endearment.

My wife is in her fifties, but she still addresses her mother as '**Amá**' and the practice is common throughout the country.

> Fuimos a visitar a mi **Amá y Apá**.

> We went to see *Mom and Dad*.

CHIQUEAR

Literal Meaning: to make small

WHO doesn't like to be pampered? But when our families or others overindulge us, we may become spoiled.

> No me gusta que mis hijos pasen mucho tiempo con sus abuelos;
>   los **chiquean** demasiado.

> I don't like it when my kids spend a lot of time with their grandparents;
>   they *spoil* them rotten.

GRANDE

Literal Meaning: big

IF someone told you that their parents were *big*, what would you imagine? That they were famous? Or would you think size? Were they over six feet tall? Did they have an obesity issue? Here *big* just means old.

> Mis papás ya están **grandes**.

> My parents are now *up in years*.

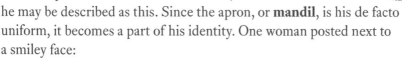

MANDILÓN

LITERAL MEANING: BIG APRÓN

WHO does the bulk of the household chores in your home? If it's the husband, he may be described as this. Since the apron, or **mandil**, is his de facto uniform, it becomes a part of his identity. One woman posted next to a smiley face:

Necesito un **mandilón** en mi vida.

In my life I need *a man tied to my apron strings*.

CARE

ASÍ, SÍ BAILA MI HIJA.

LITERAL MEANING: IF THAT'S THE CASE, THEN MY DAUGHTER WILL DANCE.

THERE's nothing like an overly-protective father at the party. With eagle eyes, he inspects each young man who attempts to ask his daughter to dance. Any chap who doesn't cut the mustard is summarily dismissed. Finally, when a respectful fellow asks his permission, he concedes. If you are a finicky negotiator, when your exacting requests are finally met, just proclaim: **Así, sí baila mi hija**. Translation? *In that case, it's a deal*.

CHIFLANDO Y APLAUDIENDO

LITERAL MEANING: WHISTLING AND CLAPPING

YOUR daughter has a steady boyfriend, and you are terrified. If to your dismay, they begin making out in your presence, you might warn:

Oigan, muchachos, **chiflando y aplaudiendo**.

Hey, guys, *keep your hands—and your lips—to yourselves*.

Since whistling and clapping would be a deterrent to, ahem, other activities, it's a humorous way to encourage them to cool it.

CHILDREN

ALIVIARSE
LITERAL MEANING: TO BE RELIEVED

EXCRUCIATING labor pangs are nothing to take lightly. The end result, however, does relieve the mother. The weight of the fetus she carried for nine months has been lifted from her.

> María ya **se alivió**.
>
> María finally *gave birth*.

CHAMACO

LIKELY from the Nahuatl *chamahua*, to fatten or to grow, **chamaco** is a popular term for a child or a boy. Choose the feminine form, **chamaca**, for a girl. On the other hand, childish actions may be called **chamacadas**. See also #193, **chamaquearle**.

①   Mi **chamaco** acaba de graduarse de la prepa.
     My *boy* just graduated from high school.

②   ¡Deja de tus **chamacadas**!
     Stop *acting like a kid*!

CHILLAR
LITERAL MEANING: TO SHRIEK

WHETHER those tears of yours are of the crocodile variety or a sincere expression of your pain of heart, Mexicans prefer this melodramatic alternative to the standard Spanish **llorar**.

> Desde que perdió el bebé, Carmen no puede hacer más que **chillar**.
>
> Since she lost the baby, Carmen has been unable to stop *crying*.

2 27

CHAVO
LITERAL MEANING: COIN

AT LEAST in Caribbean Spanish, **chavos** are coins. But in Mexico they are *children*, likely to cost you more than a coin or two.

① Tengo cinco **chavos**.
I have five *kids*.

② Mi hija es demasiada **chava** para tener novio.
My daughter is too *young* for a boyfriend.

2 28

CHILPAYATE

Another Nahuatl import, **chilpayate** denotes a child of tender age or a baby, as evidenced by this mother's tweet:

① Me toca viajar sola con un **chilpayate** hiperactivo de 13 kilos en mis piernas por tres horas. ¡Dame paciencia!
I have to travel alone with a hyperactive, 13-kilo *little boy* on my lap for three hours. Give me patience!

Another wrote:

② Se me está antojando tener un **chilpayate**, señal inequívoca de que se me está pasando el tren.
I feel like having a *baby*, a clear indication that my possibilities of marriage have all but vanished.

2 29

CUATE
LITERAL MEANING: [NAHUATL] SERPENT OR TWIN

A **cuate** is either a twin or a good buddy.

Pablo y yo somos **cuates**.

Pablo and I are *best buds*.

101

2 30

ESCUINCLE
LITERAL MEANING: BALD DOG

FOR the Aztecs the **escuincle** was a hairless breed of dog. Perhaps because most babies enter the world bald, the term was later applied to them. If only we could teach them how to fetch.

> Se fueron al Gabacho para que la mamá diera a luz; así el **escuincle** tendrá doble nacionalidad.
>
> They went to the US so that the mother could give birth; that way the *kid* would have dual nationality.

 2 31

HACER SUS PININOS
LITERAL MEANING: TO MAKE LITTLE FEETIES

IT is a moment to be photographed: the baby's first steps. With this phrase you can mark your first anything.

> Raúl está **haciendo sus pininos** como abogado.
>
> Raúl is making his very *first steps* as a lawyer.

 2 32

HUERCO

BOYS will be boys, and that means mischief. In fact, in English we sometimes refer to problematic children as hellions. It's no surprise that this Northern Mexican term for boy comes from the Latin *Orcus*, Roman god of the underworld, and by extension, the underworld itself.

① Desde **huerco** le ha gustado el fútbol.
Since he was a *kid*, he liked soccer.

② De **huerquilla** me daba miedo la oscuridad; hoy me dan miedo los recibos de la luz.
When I was a *girl* I was afraid of the dark; today I am afraid of the light bills.

2 | 33 |

PLEBE
LITERAL MEANING: COMMON PEOPLE

Here's yet another term from Northern Mexico for a young person.

① Desde **plebe** me ha gustado la aventura.
Since I was *young* I've liked adventure.

② **Plebes**, mándenle buenas vibras a mi mamá para que ya se recupere.
Hey, *guys*, send some good cheer to my mom so that she gets better.

ENDEARMENT
---

2 | 34 |

CARNAL
LITERAL MEANING: FLESHLY

OUR family is our flesh and blood, as evidenced by this meaty vocative.

① No, amor, no sé dónde anda mi **carnal**.
No, dear, I don't know where my *brother* is.

② Gracias, **carnal**, por la deliciosa cena.
Thanks, *bud*, for that delicious supper.

CHIHUAHUA'S UNUSUAL FRIEND

You've likely noticed that many of the terms for *boy* in Mexico are synonymous with good friends. Of course, the actual Spanish word for *friend* is **amigo**. Just be aware of its alternate meaning in Chihuahua: a *plunger*. A woman who had moved from Chihuahua to Mexico City one day awoke to a clogged toilet. She called the neighbor to ask for a plunger. The translated dialogue was:

—Hi, my toilet is clogged. Do you have a friend you could lend me?
—What kind of friend?
—The kind that unplugs toilets.
—He'd really have to be a friend to help you!

In said circumstances, ask for an **amigo** in Chihuahua, but everywhere else, request a **destapador** or **bomba para destapar caños**. Otherwise, you may start feeling flushed.

103

CHAPARRO

LITERAL MEANING: CHUBBY

"SHORT people ain't got no reason to live," sang Randy Newman in the 1977 hit. The less-than-tall will vigorously disagree. In either case, select this term to describe the vertically challenged. They won't be offended, because for Mexicans **chaparro** is a term of endearment and a common nickname. One notorious drug lord was even known by a shortened form: **El Chapo**; the not-so-intimidating English equivalent is *Shortie*. One young lady lamented:

> Ser alta es chido hasta que te enamoras de un **chaparrito**.

> It's cool to be tall until you fall in love with a *shortie*.

HI, FATTY!

Imagine saying that to your significant other! As cultural idiosyncrasies would have it, though, it's completely acceptable in Mexican Spanish. Husbands and wives regularly call one another **Gordo** and **Gorda** as terms of endearment. They might also call their son or daughter **Mi Gordito** or **Mi Gordita**. At least linguistically, there's no prejudice against the well-endowed. Those calories might get you some love after all.

HOME

BOTE

LITERAL MEANING: BOAT

WHERE do you place your rubbish? Likely in a trash can. In standard Spanish that's a **cesta de basura**; but here it's a **bote**. In the penal justice system, it refers to the figurative rubbish bin where criminals are held: jail.

① Oigan, muchachos. ¿Qué se hizo el **bote** de basura?
   Hey, boys. What happened to the *trash can*?

② Alfredo ya no vive aquí; lo metieron al **bote**.
   Alfredo doesn't live here anymore; they put him in the *slammer*.

| 2 | 37 |

CHAPA
LITERAL MEANING: SHEET OF METAL

WANT to feel safe? Then change the **chapas**, or locks, on your doors.

Ayer intentaron robar en la casa donde vivo. Nos dijeron que cambiáramos las **chapas** de las puertas.

Yesterday they tried to steal in the house where I live. They told us to change the *locks* on the doors.

| 2 | 38 |

RECÁMARA
LITERAL MEANING: CHAMBER OF FIREARM

WHAT part of the house to you sleep in? Probably the bedroom. Throughout most of Latin America, you might call it a **dormitorio**, **cuarto** or **habitación**. But the term of choice in Mexico is **recámara**: the chamber. Shut-eye never sounded so elegant.

Esta casa tiene tres **recámaras** y dos baños completos.

This house has three *bedrooms* and two full baths.

| 2 | 39 |

TARJA
LITERAL MEANING: TALLY STICK

PITY the beleaguered family member who spends most of their time here; the **tarja** is the local term for *kitchen sink*.

Hay que tallar bien la **tarja** y luego secarla.

You have to scrub the *kitchen sink* well and then dry it.

RESIDENCE

| 2 | 40 |

EJIDO
LITERAL MEANING: COMMUNITY LAND FOR CATTLE OR THRESHING

BEFORE the 1910 Mexican Revolution, a small number of wealthy Mexicans and foreigners owned the majority of the country's farmland. Gradually over the following decades, the government allotted large parcels, or **ejidos**, to community groups. However, community members had usufruct rights only, meaning they could use the land and get fruit, or profit, from it. Then, in 1992, President Carlos Salinas de Gortari modified the Constitution, paving the way for **ejidos** to be privatized. Even so, the term persists in place names in rural areas, a reminder of Mexico's checkered land reform history.

> Los papás de Laura acaban de comprar un terreno en el **Ejido** Carmen Serdán.

> Laura's parents just bought a property in the Carmen Serdán *Development*.

FINCAR
LITERAL MEANING: TO FARM

STANDARD Spanish judges a farm to be a **finca**. That's why you might link this verb to agriculture. Here, though, it just means *to build* and implies house construction. In this sense you can *farm* even in the heart of a metropolis.

> Javier y Laura **fincaron** en Chimalhuacán.

> Javier and Laura *built their house* in Chimalhuacán.

FRACCIONAMIENTO
LITERAL MEANING: THE FRACTION THING

TAKE your pizza and slice it into eight pieces. In so doing, you have fractionated the pie. In the same way, when developers divvy up and sell off a property piece by piece, it's known as a **fraccionamiento**.

> Jorge vive en el **fraccionamiento** El Tecojote.

> Jorge lives in the El Tejocote *neighborhood*.

In everyday speech, it's often abbreviated to just **frac**.

> Compré la pizza aquí mismo en el **frac**.

> I bought the pizza right here in the neighborhood.

7

Food for Thought

BREAD & PASTA
---

2 43

¿A QUIÉN LE DAN PAN QUE LLORE?

LITERAL MEANING: WHO CRIES WHEN YOU GIVE THEM BREAD?

A man stands on a street corner passing out free bread. What if an ungrateful person, after receiving his loaf, turns and complains: "Hey, this is a little dry!"? What gall! Consequently, select this popular phrase to express gratitude for any freebies that come your way. It's on par with: *Who looks a gift horse in the mouth?*

2 44

SOPA FRÍA

LITERAL MEANING: COLD SOUP

NEWLY arrived in Mexico, I was at a meal when someone asked me to pass the **sopa fría**. My eyes scanned up and down the table, but not a glimmer of soup. Baffled and silently wondering what poor soul would desire cold soup, I observed as someone grabbed a macaroni salad and passed it. A completely liquid-less soup? Who would have thunk it?

Me encantó la **sopa fría** que hizo mi tía.

I loved that *macaroni salad* that my aunt made.

CONTAINERS
---

2 45

CHAROLA

WANT to display those tasty hors d'oeuvres on a shiny platter? Then here you won't place them on a **bandeja**, the standard term, but rather, a **charola**. Just make sure you don't break the law. Otherwise, a police office may arrive and flash his **charola**, or *badge*.

① ¡Qué **charola** más chula!

What a beautiful *platter*!

② Al llegar al lugar de los hechos, el policía mostró su **charola**.

Upon arriving at the crime scene, the officer showed his *badge*.

`2` `46`

ITACATE

LITERAL MEANING: [NAHUATL] STOMACH

WAS the food ever so succulent that you wished you had two stomachs? With the **itacate**, now you can. How so? When a party ends, the host may realize that he made too much food. Remedy? He hastily prepares little doggie bags of leftovers and hands them out to departing guests. Such gift bags were called **itacates**, essentially a second stomach. Whatever its form, the word persists in everyday speech, though the emphasis has shifted from the container to its contents. A Mexican may invite you to an excursion at a park and add:

No te olvides de traer tu **itacate**.

Don't forget to bring *something to eat*.

`2` `47`

SALIRSE DEL HUACAL

LITERAL MEANING: TO LEAVE THE FOOD CONTAINER

AS we learned in term #43, a **huacal** was a wooden container where dishes could be washed. But that wasn't its only purpose. It also served as a storage bin for fruits and sometimes live animals. But if the animal wasn't tied to the container, he might wiggle his way out. Now you've got a problem. Similarly today, when in Mexican Spanish someone leaves their figurative **huacal**, they've gone too far and mattters are out of hand. Internet news portal *Mundo Real* observed:

Esta semana, en el aeropuerto que todavía ni empieza y ya ha tenido más tropezones que Bambi, los precios **se salieron del huacal**.

This week, in the airport whose construction has not yet begun and which has stumbled more than Bambi, prices *have gotten out of control*.

UNICEL

Literal Meaning: one cell

OCCASIONALLY a brand name over time gains so much recognition that it becomes a proper noun. Need a disposable cup for coffee on the go? If so, you might ask for a styrofoam cup. In reality, styrofoam is a brand name for polystyrene foam. **Unicel**, also a brand name, means the same locally.

¿Me podrías dar el café en un **unicel** por favor?

Could you give me the coffee in a *styrofoam cup* please?

DAIRY

CUANDO TÚ VAS POR LA LECHE, YO YA VOY RODANDO LOS QUESOS.

Literal Meaning: When you go for the milk, I am already rolling the cheeses.

FANCY crafting your own cheddar cheese? Hope you have oodles of time. Even mild cheddar could take from two to three months to age. If you are barely leaving to buy the milk, you haven't even started yet. Milk this saying for all it's worth when your spouse or close friend suggests something you thought of long ago. It's the equivalent of: *I'm way ahead of you!*

ECHAR MUCHA CREMA A LOS TACOS

Literal Meaning: to throw a lot of cream on the tacos

A LITTLE sour cream on those tacos adds a nice touch. But too much can ruin them. If you go overboard in any sense, you may be criticized with:

¡Bájale! Estás **echando mucha crema a los tacos**.

Tone it down a notch! You are *exaggerating*.

2 51

EL QUE CON LECHE SE QUEMA, HASTA EL JOCOQUE SOPLA.

LITERAL MEANING: HE WHO BURNS HIMSELF WITH MILK, EVEN BLOWS ON THE YOGURT.

THE sun has yet to show its face on a cold winter morning, but before your farm chores, you've got time for some hot milk and bread. Not realizing how scalding hot the frothy mixture is, you take your first sip like it's water.
Big mistake! Now you've burned your tongue and palate. The following day at the same time, you decide on **jocoque**, a buttermilk-based creation similar to yogurt. Keenly aware of the previous day's debacle, before you take your first bite, you blow on it, even though **jocoque** is served cold. The problem? You are gun shy.

> Desde que se divorció, Enrique no ha querido volver a noviar. **El que con leche se quema, hasta el jocoque sopla**.
>
> Since his divorce, Enrique has had no desire to date anyone. *Once bitten, twice shy.*

DRINKS

---

2 52

CAGUAMA

LITERAL MEANING: SPECIES OF TURTLE

READY for a cold beer on a hot day? What size? A can? A bottle? If you're really parched, you might splurge on a **caguama**. What's that? It's a bottle just shy of a liter, 940 ml! That's nearly the equivalent of two pints. Before the 1960s they called this presentation *family size*. However, in northern Mexico the natives treasured a popular dish which included **caguama** turtle meat. The turtle's color matched the large brown jars nicely, and the bottle size got its nickname, now widely used throughout the country. One man yearned:

> ¡Qué ganas de una **caguama** en este calor!
>
> With this heat I'd die for a *family-size bottle of beer*!

CHELA

LITERAL MEANING: BLONDE WOMAN

SINCE beer has a golden sheen, it's like a blonde woman with a twinkle in her eye, according to this term. From **chela** comes the mixed drink **michelada**, a refreshing combo of beer, lime juice and spices. **Michelada** is a contraction of **mi chela helada**, that is, *my cold beer*.

Hoy tomé mi primera **chela** en dos meses.

Today I drank my first *beer* in two months.

CHISGUETE

LITERAL MEANING: A SMALL AMOUNT OF LIQUOR

ARE there just a few drops of precious liquid left? Then it's a mere **chisguete**. Opt for this noun to describe meager quantities of any liquid.

① En unos minutos caerá otro **chisguete** de agua.
   In a few minutes another *light shower* will fall.

② ¿Quieres el último **chisguete** del café?
   Do want the last *few drops* of coffee?

PAJARETE

LITERAL MEANING: FINE, AROMATIC WINE

DARE to dabble in drinks? Then visit rural Jalisco and ask for a **pajarete**. What's the recipe? Go to a dairy farm early morning when they are milking the cows. In a cup add a swig or more of typical sugar cane liquor. Next, mix in ground chocolate and a little sugar. Finally, take the cup and stick it right under the udder, filling it to the brim with raw milk. (See **leche bronca**, in the box after term #205.) Rural folk drink this at daybreak—not for its alcoholic content—but as an energy drink. Now that's organic.

2 | 56

REFRESCOS

LITERAL MEANING: REFRESHMENTS

ACCORDING to a report in the *El Universal* daily, Mexico is ranked number one in the world in soft drink consumption; each inhabitant chugs a whopping 160 liters of the sugary concoction annually. Should you care to join them, then ask for a **refresco**. This differs from **soda** and **gaseosa** used in other Latin countries, though you will hear **soda** along the northern border.

La nueva normalidad en los aviones no incluye ni cacahuatitos ni **refrescos**.

The new normal on a plane means no peanuts and no *soft drinks*.

JUST WANT WATER?

You would think that asking for water is as easy as falling out of bed. Just ask for **agua**, right? Wrong! Why? That's because blended fruit juices are known as **aguas de sabor**, that is, flavored drinks. **Agua de horchata** is a rice drink. **Agua de melón** is a blended cantaloupe drink. And that's where the ambiguity arises. If what you're really hankering for is just plain water, ask for **agua natural**.

---

 2 | 57

REGAR EL TEPACHE

LITERAL MEANING: TO SPILL THE FERMENTED PINEAPPLE DRINK

ARE you a big talker? Eager to be the first to spread the news? If so, be careful not to spill the beans, or in this case, the **tepache**, a fermented drink made from pineapple or other fruits.

¡Híjole! ¡Ya **regaste el tepache**! Nadie más supo que mi esposa está embarazada.

Man! You *spilled the beans*! No one else knew my wife is pregnant.

 2 | 58

TENER ATOLE EN LAS VENAS

LITERAL MEANING: TO HAVE A HOT, CORN-BASED DRINK IN YOUR VEINS

HOW well do you work under pressure? Do you get frazzled? Or can you keep your cool even under the worst of duress? This anatomical idiom describes the latter. Since **atole** is a thick, corn beverage, it inches its way through your digestive system. If it circulated in your blood, it would be like antifreeze to a car.

① Mi jefe nunca pierde los estribos. **Tiene atole en las venas.**
My boss never loses his temper. *He's got nerves of steel.*

On the other hand, this virtue of not acting on impulse could render the individual slow and boring.

② Mi jefe me contesta los correos al mes. **Tiene atole en las venas.**
My boss answers my emails a month later. *It's like watching paint dry.*

FRUITS

NOT YOUR ORDINARY FRUIT

EVER been judged as ordinary, run-of-the-mill? Then maybe you can sympathize with the under-appreciated apricot. Standard Spanish chose to call the fruit the elegant Arabic-based **albaricoque**. On the other hand, María Moliner in her *Diccionario del uso del español* points out that **chabacano** has the additional meaning of "a trifle,  something of little or no value." Perhaps early settlers deemed the apricot less impressive than cantaloupes, grapes, and other fruits. *Food and Travel México* advises:

Encontrar un **chabacano** en su punto es una odisea frutal que al final puede no ser tan exitosa.

Finding an *apricot* at just the right ripeness is a fruity odyssey that in the end may prove unsuccessful.

FRESA
Literal Meaning: strawberry

HOW do you prefer your shortcake? Likely with strawberries on top. If social status were a shortcake, the elite and up-and-coming would be the strawberries, or as expressed in local Spanish, the **fresas**. Affected speech characterizes these socialites, who are either wealthy or pretend to be so. Just as the Valley Girls of the 1980s would, like, gag you with a spoon, these snobs insert **o sea** (that is) into most sentences. Put off by the snooty pronunciation and word choice? You might respond with: **¡Sácate la papa de la boca!** *Take the potato out of your mouth.*

Beatriz se cree una **fresa**; solo compra en tiendas de marca.

Beatriz thinks she's *high-class*; she only buys from brand-name stores.

2 60

PERO TÚ NO VENDES PIÑAS.
LITERAL MEANING: BUT YOU DON'T SELL PINEAPPLE.

APPARENTLY before the strawberries climbed to the top of the social ladder, pineapples, or at least their sellers, were a grade above the rest, as per this comeback.

A: Esa mujer está refea.	A: That woman is super ugly.
B: **Pero tú no vendes piñas**.	B: *That's the pot calling the kettle black.*

2 61

¿QUIERES QUE TE LO EXPLIQUE CON PERAS Y MANZANAS?
LITERAL MEANING: DO YOU WANT ME TO EXPLAIN IT TO YOU WITH PEARS AND APPLES?

VAGUELY recall your first-grade math classes? At that age simple addition and subtraction seemed like rocket science. To simplify matters for the stupefied, teachers resorted to fruit comparisons. "If Johnny has five apples and gives you two, how many does Johnny have left?" Suddenly, subtraction was demystified. If, then, a superior must explain a concept with pears and apples, the implication is that your mind is still in first grade.

A: No entiendo.

B: **¿Quieres que te lo explique con peras y manzanas?**

A: I don't understand.

B: *Do I have to spell it out for you?*

GLUTTONY

ATRACADO

Literal Meaning: to bring alongside or dock a boat

BOATS can haul an enormous amount of cargo. If you devour boatloads of food, then you might describe your condition with this maritime adjective.

No puedo comer ni un bocado más. Estoy **atracado**.

I can't eat another bite. I'm *stuffed*.

COMERSE EL MANDADO

Literal Meaning: to eat the errand

YOUR mother has sent you for groceries, but boy are you hungry! On the way home, you can't resist and start nibbling. When you arrive, there's little left of the purchase. Pick this idiom when a competitor beats you to the punch.

Cuando murió mi mamá, mi hermano se adelantó a poner el titúlo de su coche a su nombre. **Se comió el mandado**.

When my mom died, my brother jumped ahead and put the title of her car in his name. *He beat me to the punch*.

GRAINS & SEEDS

ANDAR COMO PEPITA EN COMAL

Literal Meaning: to walk like a pumpkin seed on a griddle

PUT a pumpkin seed on a hot griddle and it will gyrate like a break dancer. Too much to do? Impatient? Anxious? Then this describes you to a tee.

En mi edificio, mis vecinos **andan como pepita en comal** todo el día para adentro y para afuera... lamentable.

In my building my neighbors *are running around like chickens with their heads cut off*, in and out all day. How sad!

ESE ARROZ YA SE COCIÓ.

LITERAL MEANING: THAT RICE IS ALREADY COOKED.

COOKING rice takes time, but when it's done, it's done. Single out this culinary saying to signal a done deal. See also #275, **Ya se hizo la machaca**.

A: ¿Ya abrieron otra vez los gimnasios?

B: **Ese arroz ya se coció**.

A: Did they open the gyms again?

B: *That's a done deal.*

IMPORTARLE UN CACAHUATE

LITERAL MEANING: TO CARE ABOUT A PEANUT

While the majority of Spanish speakers snack on **maní**, or peanuts, here they are called **cacahuates**. Since a solitary peanut pales in significance, if a person alleges that something's worth a peanut to them, then it's worthless.

Pueden decir lo que quieran. **Me importa un cacahuate**.

You can say what you want. *I couldn't care less.*

NO SE PUEDE CHIFLAR Y COMER PINOLE.

LITERAL MEANING: YOU CAN'T WHISTLE AND EAT CORN MEAL.

MULTI-TASKERS beware! There are certain activities that you can't perform simultaneously, as this popular adage asserts. If you had **pinole**, a sweetened corn meal, in your mouth, it would be impossible to whistle. Tab this corny logic when someone attempts the impossible or inadvisable without visualizing the big picture.

Quieren acabar con el virus y abrir la economía al mismo tiempo. **No se puede chiflar y comer pinole**.

They want to erradicate the virus and open the economy at the same time. *You can't do two things at once.*

SER EL AJONJOLÍ DE TODOS LOS MOLES

LITERAL MEANING: TO BE THE SESAME SEED OF ALL MOLE SAUCES

MEXICO'S **mole** sauce is internationally renowned. The bitterness of the chocolate, the bite of peppers, the acidity of tomatoes, the pungency of garlic—together with any number of select ingredients—combine to make **mole** a gastronomic delight. But **moles** are like snowflakes; no two are alike. Even so, sesame seeds are the common denominator; they're in the majority of variations. Logically, if someone is considered the sesame seed of all sauces, they are staples of the social scene. I once asked a woman her religious affiliation. Her answer will be forever burned into my memory:

> Yo he sido católica, evangélica, y mormona; he sido **el ajonjolí de todos los moles**.
>
> I was Catholic, Evangelical, and Mormon; I've been *a social butterfly*.

MEALS

ALMUERZO

LITERAL MEANING: LUNCH

FORGET everything you ever learned about meal names in Spanish. You know the drill. **Desayuno** = breakfast; **almuerzo** = lunch; and **cena** = supper. Wrong, wrong, and right. Erase the first two from your memory. Conjure up instead the life of a farmer. He would wake before sunrise and nibble on something just to get started. That was breakfast. At about 10 in the morning after milking the cows, he returns with a ferocious appetite. It was time for lunch, **almuerzo**, but what Anglo speakers would equate more with brunch. Then he was back to the grind. By 2 or 3 o'clock in the afternoon, again famished, he returns for the **comida**. Again to his chores and in the evening at 6 or later, he can now enjoy his **cena**.

① Roberto salió con Raquel al **almuerzo**.
Roberto went out with Raquel for *brunch*.

② Fuimos a la casa de los Rodríguez para la **comida**.
We went to the Rodriguez's for *lunch*.

COMIDA CORRIDA

Literal Meaning: run-off food

BY the sounds of it, you might imagine this to be fast food. Instead, a **comida corrida** is a menu option at small family restaurants called **fondas**. It's a plate with a main course and two or three entrées. Usually the individual elements are predetermined, which makes the offering affordable. After her meal, a satisfied customer gushed:

Hoy conocí este lugar que me encantó, con **comida corrida de cuatro tiempos**.

Today I found this place that I loved; they had a *four-course combo meal*.

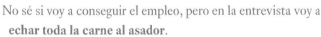

MEATS

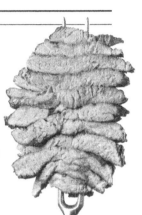

ECHAR TODA LA CARNE AL ASADOR

Literal Meaning: to throw all the meat on the grill

GRILLING meat is a great Mexican pastime. If guests are waiting, would you throw just one measly piece at a time on the grill? Of course, not. You have to go all in.

No sé si voy a conseguir el empleo, pero en la entrevista voy a **echar toda la carne al asador**.

I don't know if I'll get the job, but in the interview I'm going *to give it all I got*.

ECHARSE UN TACO

Literal Meaning: to throw oneself a taco

ARE you between meals and yet still have the munchies? Then follow this phrase's counsel. It's not exclusive to eating tacos, just getting a bite to eat.

Vamos a **echarnos un taco**.

Let's *get a bite to eat*.

PERSEGUIR LA CHULETA

LITERAL MEANING: TO CHASE THE PORK CHOP

WORKING hard for a living? Then you are pursuing the figurative pork chop.

> Es sábado y tengo sueño, pero ni modo. Hay que **perseguir la chuleta**.
>
> It's Saturday and I'm sleepy, but whatever. You've got *to bring home the bacon*.

This phrase also appears as **corretear la chuleta**, literally, to run after the pork chop. In either case, you don't have to live high on the hog to follow the pork chop; you just have to make ends meet.

QUESADILLA

LITERAL MEANING: THE LITTLE CHEESE THING

IN its basic form, a **quesadilla** is a tortilla folded in half and filled with cheese. However, in the Mexico City area, any folded and filled tortilla concoction is considered a **quesadilla**—with or without cheese.

> Es la hora del café, con su respectiva **quesadilla**.
>
> It's coffee time, including the requisite *fried, filled tortilla*.

YA SE HIZO LA MACHACA.

LITERAL MEANING: THE DRIED BEEF AND PORK MEAT IS ALREADY DONE.

THE hot, arid climate of Northern Mexico lends itself to the drying of beef and pork for later consumption. Given that the meat dehydration process takes hours, when finally completed, it's a relief. Pick this saying if something positive has come to fruition, especially after great effort.

> Julio ya le pidió la mano a Melisa y ella dijo que sí. ¡**Ya se hizo la machaca**!
>
> Julio asked Melisa to marry him and she said yes. *It's a done deal!*

SAUCES

| 2 | 76 |

¡A DARLE, QUE ES MOLE DE OLLA!
LITERAL MEANING: LET'S HIT IT! IT'S MOLE SAUCE FROM THE POT!

NEED to prod someone to get a move on? Then add this to your repertoire. **Mole** is the iconic chocolate-and-chili sauce, but **mole de olla** is something completely different, a fatty beef soup. As it cools, the grease begins to congeal; cold, it looks disgusting. To enjoy it you have to eat it quickly. Something similar happens in our work; the faster and more earnestly we do it, the better. If you want to cheer on your co-workers or if you are in oversight and wish to goad on your employees, just fire off this hearty saying. An alternative with the same meaning is: ¡**En caliente, porque se hace sebo!**.

| 2 | 77 |

MERO MOLE
LITERAL MEANING: THE VERY MOLE SAUCE

WHAT is your expertise? What are you passionate about? Whatever it may be, for Mexicans it's your **mero mole**.

① Eso es tu **mero mole**, amiga: vino y libros.
That's your *passion*, my friend: wine and books.

② Algunos museos han ofrecido recorridos virtuales. Eso es mi **mero mole**.
Some musuems offer virtual tours. That's *right up my alley*.

SNACKS

| 2 | 78 |

BOTANA
LITERAL MEANING: A PATCH FOR WINESKINS

ORIGINALLY a patch for wineskins, today you might munch on a **botana** to patch your hunger.

¿Qué quieren de **botana**?

What would you like as an *appetizer*?

GUZGOS

Literal Meaning: gluttony

YOU just ate, but those hunger pangs won't go away. Or maybe you're attempting to eat away your sorrows. Either way, you've got a case of these.

① ¡Cuidado con los **guzgos**!
Watch out for those *cravings*!

② No sé por qué, pero tengo los **guzgos**.
I don't know why, but I've got the *munchies*.

TOMA PA' TUS CHUCHULUCOS.

Literal Meaning: Take this for your goodies.

GRANDMA and grandpa went out of their way to win over our affections. When they visited, they may have reached into their pockets and pulled out a few bucks for you. It is as if they were saying: 'Buy yourself something nice with this.' Summon this Mexican equivalent to make friends with the kids you meet. Hand over your spare change with a friendly: **Toma pa' tus chuchulucos.**

SOUPS

DEL AÑO DEL CALDO

Literal Meaning: from soup year

IN what year did your great grandparents get married? Do you even know their names? If an event happened that long ago, then natives will say it happened in the Year of Soup's Invention.

① Sí, mija, eso fue en el **año del caldo**; ya cállate.
Yes, my dear friend, but *that's old news*. Shut up already.

② Dejen de mirar esas fotos; son **del año del caldo**.
Stop looking at those pictures; they're *super old*.

2 82

HACER CHUC
LITERAL MEANING: [MAYAN] TO MAKE SOFT

DON'T throw out that dry bread! Why not dip it in your soup or your coffee? That's what's suggested in the Mayan verb *ch'uuk*, to loosen something tight. Try out this idiom on your next visit to Cancún.

¡No **hagas chuc** en mi sopa!

Don't *dip your bread* in my soup!

SUPER-SIZE YOUR ORDER—MAYAN STYLE

Want to make sure that delicious **torta** is served with all the fixings? Or that your **pozole** is filled to the brim? Then try out this phrase in the Yucatán: **Sírvemelo bien nohoch**. **Nohoch** in Mayan means *fat*. Locals will happily comply.

---

2 83

MENUDO
LITERAL MEANING: SMALL

HERE'S the term for cow stomach soup. Need I say more?

No me gusta comer **menudo**; por lo menos, no muy a menudo.

I don't like *beef tripe soup*; at least, not very often.

2 84

SALE MÁS CARO EL CALDO QUE LAS ALBÓNDIGAS.
LITERAL MEANING: THE BROTH ENDS UP BEING
MORE EXPENSIVE THAN THE MEATBALLS.

WE live in a throwaway society. In developed countries, who gets their shoes repaired? Who pays to get a printer fixed? In many cases, repair costs are prohibitive; it's more feasible to buy a new item. Order up this saying when faced with unreasonable repair costs. It's an able substitute for: *The cure is worse than the disease.*

TORTILLAS

A FALTA DE PAN, TORTILLAS.

LITERAL MEANING: FOR THE LACK OF BREAD, TORTILLAS.

NO bread? No problem. Eat tortillas instead. Settle on this saying when you have to improvise with what's available.

> Quería salir al cine, pero me quedé viendo la tele. **A falta de pan, tortillas**.

> I wanted to go to the movies, but ended up staying and watching TV. *I had to make do.*

GRINGA

LITERAL MEANING: AMERICAN WOMAN

URBAN legend has it that two American girls studying in Mexico City in the 1960s frequented a taco shop. One day they made an unusual petition: that their tacos al pastor be prepared in a flour tortilla with cheese. Other customers noticed and started asking that their order be served **a la gringa**, or *Gringo-style*. Essentially a **gringa** is a two-tortilla sandwich.

> Dame dos órdenes de **gringas al pastor**, por favor.

> Please give me two orders of *pork and cheese sandwiched between two tortillas.*

THE TORTILLA BIAS

All tortillas are not created equal. So much is that the case that in northern Mexico we find this preferential saying: **Si son de maíz, ni las mientes; si son de harina, ni las calientes**. This literally translates to: *If they are corn, don't even mention them; if they are flour, don't bother heating them up*. Enough said.

TLAYUDA

FAMED in the southern state of Oaxaca, the **tlayuda** is the mother of all tortillas. The more than 12-inch diameter serves as a base for a variety of meats and cheeses and is toasted to perfection. One is a complete meal.

`2 88`

TOTOPO

NACHOS have become popular in the US, either as a tasty snack at the movie theater or a menu item at a Mexican restaurant. But in Mexico the chips themselves are called **totopos**.

Mi parte favorita es ir a los restaurantes y comer **totopos**.

My favorite thing is going to restaurants and eating *tortilla chips*.

UTENSILS

`2 89`

METATE

LITERAL MEANING: [NAHUATL] HAND STONE

EVER make something from scratch? It takes time and loads of elbow grease. Just ask the Mexican women who have wielded a **metate**; that's the large flat stone seen here. The smaller piece on top is the **metlalpil**. Together they make a dynamic duo that transforms steamy corn kernels into the prime material for pure tortilla glory. A good friend of ours made the best **mole** ever with these simple instruments.

Hoy hice mole. Solo admito que usé la licuadora y no el **metate**.

Today I made mole sauce. But I admit I used the blender, not a *stone grinder*.

`2 90`

MOLCAJETE

LITERAL MEANING: [NAHUATL] SALSA CONTAINER

UNLIKE the flat **metate** above, the **molcajete** is a stone mortar and pestle. Its concave bowl is perfect for creating spicy salsas and other condiments.

Por fin me compré un **molcajete**.

I finally bought myself a *stone mortar and pestle*.

POPOTE

LITERAL MEANING: [NAHUATL] STRAW

NEED a straw for your drink? Ask for one of these. Or don't.

> Para proteger el medio ambiente, pida su bebida sin **popote**.
>
> To protect the environment, ask for your drink without a *straw*.

VEGETABLES

2 92

AL NOPAL SOLO SE LE ARRIMAN CUANDO TIENE TUNAS.

LITERAL MEANING: THEY ONLY APPROACH THE CACTUS WHEN IT HAS FRUIT.

HOW many true friends do you have? When things are going well, it may be difficult to tell. Only when the storm strikes will the chaff be separated from the wheat. Just ask the solitary cactus. On a typical day his only visitor is the parching sun. But when he bears his vermilion fruit, or **tuna**, friends arrive in droves. Invoke this desert wisdom when fair-weather friends have abandoned you.

2 93

CHÍCHARO

A departure from the standard **guisante**, this is the local term for a *pea*.

> ① Mi hijo me está probando la paciencia; come sus **chícharos** uno a uno.
> My son is trying my patience; he's eating his *peas* one by one.

You might also dub an apprentice or rookie a **chícharo**, due perhaps to his pea-size experience.

> ② Dile al **chícharo** que nos ayude a dejar todo el taller limpio.
> Tell the *newbie* to help us clean up the entire shop.

2 94

DE CHILE, MOLE Y POZOLE

LITERAL MEANING: OF PEPPERS, MOLE SAUCE AND PORK-HOMINY SOUP

DO you invest in the stock market? Then you well know the benefits of diversification. If one stock tanks, another may soar. It's a baked-in protection. When you need a little bit of everything, petition it with this piquant phrase. It's a synonym for term #5, **de tocho morocho**.

A: ¿Qué vendes en el tianguis?

B: **De chile, mole y pozole**.

A: What do you sell in the street market?

B: *A little bit of everything.*

 2 95

EXTENDERSE COMO VERDOLAGA

LITERAL MEANING: TO STRETCH OUT LIKE PURSLANE

IMAGINE going to the movie theater when it is nearly empty. How much space would you occupy? You might feel inclined to put your feet up and stretch your arms over seats on either side of you. You would have the run of the place. In said circumstance, Mexicans will liken your behavior to that of the purslane, or **verdolaga**. When planted, it will extend itself in a three foot diameter, essentially taking over the area around it. One young woman reflected:

Lo bueno de la soledad es que te toca dormir **extendida como verdolaga**.

The good thing about solitude is that you get to sleep *all spread out.*

2 96

GARBANZO DE A LIBRA

LITERAL MEANING: A ONE-POUND CHICKPEA

IF a chickpea had to don gloves and enter the boxing ring, it would have to compete with the light flyweights; it would be the heaviest of underdogs. Imagine: a half cup of these rotund legumes is barely 3.5 onzes. A solitary bean would barely move the scale. Should a humble laborer in the field happen upon a one-pound chickpea, he would have discovered something truly extraordinary. One fan raved about a star soccer player in Morelia:

Ruidíaz es en Morelia un **garbanzo de a libra**; para encontrar a alguien con su efectividad y calidad, tendrías que voltear a ver a las grandes estrellas.

Ruidíaz is in Morelia a *top-notch* player; to find someone with his effectiveness and quality, you would have to turn to the biggest stars.

 2 97

HAY QUE MEDIR BIEN EL AGUA A LOS CAMOTES.

LITERAL MEANING: YOU HAVE TO MEASURE WELL THE WATER FOR THE SWEET POTATOES.

HOW much water do you pour into the pot when cooking sweet potatoes? Too much, and it will take forever; not enough, and the water will evaporate, leaving you a smoking, charred mess. If preparing tubers requires such careful calculation, what about getting married, starting a business, or other endeavors? This culinary insight reminds us to look before we leap. Feel free to substitute **frijoles**, or beans, for the sweet potatoes, with the same meaning.

A: Papá, pienso pedirle la mano a Luisa.

B: Pues, **mide bien el agua a los camotes**.

A: Dad, I'm planning to ask Luisa to marry me.

B: Well, *make sure you think things through well*.

 2 98

HUITLACOCHE

ONE man's trash is another man's treasure. Just ask the oft-maligned **huitlacoche**. This black, edible mushroom attacks corn and won't win many beauty pageants. In fact, most countries consider it a plague. But here it's gourmet fare. Compare with term #212, **caer el chahuistle**.

Se me antojan unos tacos de **huitlacoche**.

I'm in the mood for some *gourmet mushroom* tacos.

JITOMATE

LITERAL MEANING: [NAHUATL] FAT, WATER BELLY BUTTON

ARE you an innie or an outee? Pardon the belly button inquiry. As genetics and obstetric techniques would have it, we innees have a mere dimple, whereas the outees sport a small appendage. Consider the **jitomate**, or red tomato, as one of the outees. Its moniker comes from a Nahuatl root that means the *fat, water belly button*. Sometimes a navel idea is a novel idea.

¿A cómo tienen los **jitomates**?

How much are the *tomatoes*?

THE FEAR-INSPIRING TOMATO PICKERS

You're starting a new sports franchise and you need a name that will strike fear into your opponents' hearts. Tigers? Lions? Sharks? Devils? In Culiacán, Sinaloa none of those were chosen for the baseball team. Instead, they are known as the mighty Culiacán **Tomateros**, or Tomato Pickers! Pass the salsa.

PARIR CHAYOTES

LITERAL MEANING: TO GIVE BIRTH TO A PRICKLY SQUASH

THE pangs of childbirth can be excruciating. The expectant mother sweats bullets and breathes as if to participate in a cardio video. All of that anguish is the sacrifice to welcome a cuddly  baby to the world. But what if a person had to give birth to a prickly chayote squash? That would be an entirely new level of pain. Call on this phrase when the going gets tough.

Antes era fácil para Miguel encontrar empleo en todos lados, pero ahora con la pandemia está **pariendo chayotes**.

Before it was easy for Miguel to find work anywhere, but now during the pandemic he's *in dire straits*.

Since **chayotes** are a rotund vegetable, figuratively they represent the fat payouts given to TV and radio stations to play certain content or bribes of any kind given to politicians.

Los **chayotes** secuestran la verdad.

Bribes kidnap the truth.

TRAGAR CAMOTE
LITERAL MEANING: TO SWALLOW SWEET POTATO

GIVEN the sweet potato's dense, starchy consistency, you have to chew it well and swallow hard for it to go down. When we are called onto the carpet for our words, we may also swallow hard and begin to stammer.

Cuando los reporteros cuestionaron la factibilidad del plan del gobierno,
el gobernador comenzó a **tragar camote**.

When reporters began to question the viability of the government's plan,
the governor began *to stammer*.

TRONAR COMO EJOTE
LITERAL MEANING: TO THUNDER LIKE A STRING BEAN

EVER snapped a freshly plucked string bean? The clean, swift break elicits a distinctive crack—not unlike having a bone broken in one fell swoop. Pick this veggie analogy when warning of complete failure. As we learned in the box under term #95, when an appliance breaks, Mexicans will announce that it **tronó**, or thundered. If that break is like a string bean, then it will be a complete and total failure. A perspective employer asked one woman if she was familiar with advanced features of Microsoft Excel. Bluffing, she claimed she did, then admitted:

Si me hace el examen ahora, voy a **tronar como ejote**, pero ya qué.

If he gives me the test right now, I am going *to fail miserably*, but so what.

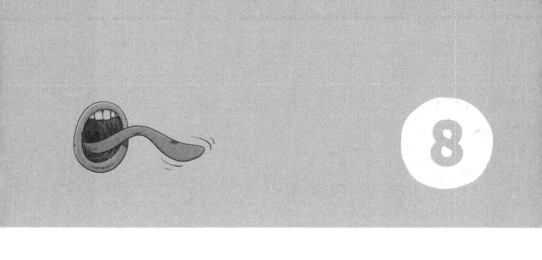

8

Mexico Inside Out

CITIES

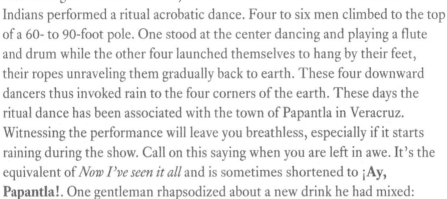

3 | **03**

¡AY, PAPANTLA, TUS HIJOS VUELAN!

LITERAL MEANING: WOE, PAPANTLA, YOUR SONS ARE FLYING!

NEED some rain? You'll have to do more than bribe your meteorologist. In ancient times, the Totonac and Huastec Indians performed a ritual acrobatic dance. Four to six men climbed to the top of a 60- to 90-foot pole. One stood at the center dancing and playing a flute and drum while the other four launched themselves to hang by their feet, their ropes unraveling them gradually back to earth. These four downward dancers thus invoked rain to the four corners of the earth. These days the ritual dance has been associated with the town of Papantla in Veracruz. Witnessing the performance will leave you breathless, especially if it starts raining during the show. Call on this saying when you are left in awe. It's the equivalent of *Now I've seen it all* and is sometimes shortened to ¡**Ay, Papantla!**. One gentleman rhapsodized about a new drink he had mixed:

> Me hice un agua de uva con tuna que ¡**ay, Papantla!**.
>
> I made a blended drink of grapes and cactus fruit that *was out of this world!*

3 | **04**

CACHANILLA

LITERAL MEANING: NAME OF PLANT

IN Baja California grows the **cachanilla**, a broad-leafed plant (*Pluchea sericea*), which early settlers of Mexicali—just across the border from Calexico, California—fashioned into huts. In time, the town's inhabitants adopted the primitive building material as their nickname. It was further cemented into the language with Antonio Váldez Herrera's popular 1963 song *Soy pura cachanilla*, that is, I'm 100% from Mexicali.

> Mi tío es **cachanilla** y cada vez que viene nos trae chiles rellenos de mariscos.
>
> My uncle is *from Mexicali* and every trip home he brings seafood-stuffed peppers.

CHILANGO

MEET the peppery demonym for Mexico City residents. Though the official term is **capitalino**, a nod to their status as denizens of the nation's capital, **chilango** has soared in popularity. In the eyes of outsiders it was a slur towards the uppity. Even so, what began as an insult is now a source of pride. Since 2003 the chic magazine *Chilango* has circulated, championing the virtues of **Chilangolandia**—Mexico City.

Mi nuevo profesor tiene acento **chilango**.

My new teacher has a *Mexico City* accent.

GOODBYE, D.F.

It used to be that residents of the greater Mexico City area were called **defeños**, a reference to the **Distrito Federal (D.F.)**. However, on January 19, 2016, the Federal District was officially dissolved, paving the way for Mexico City to function as a special entity. It's now known by its new acronym: **CDMX**.

CULICHE

CÉSAR Millan, the world-famous dog whisperer, is a **culiche**, a native of Culiacán, the largest city in the state of Sinaloa.

Las bodas **culiches** comienzan tarde y van hasta después de la medianoche.

Weddings *in Culiacán* start late and go on until after midnight.

ES DE PROVINCIA.

LITERAL MEANING: HE'S FROM A PROVINCE.

CITY slickers may turn up their noses at country bumpkins. If you are Mexican, but not from Mexico City, the natives will say this of you—never mind that the country is divided into states, not provinces.

Mi nuevo vecino **es de provincia**.

My new neighbor is *from out of town*. [Possible implication: *from the boonies*.]

JAROCHO

LITERAL MEANING: ILL-MANNERED

IN 1519 Spanish conquistador Hernán Cortés founded a city that he called **La Villa Rica de la Vera Cruz**, literally *The Rich Town of the True Cross*. Today, it's called the Port of Veracruz, and its inhabitants bear the nickname **jarochos**.

¡Cuánto anhelo un café **jarocho**!

How I yearn for a *Veracruz* coffee!

NEZA YORK

WITH a whopping nine syllables in its name, Ciudad Nezahualcóyotl is a mouthful. What's the solution to pronouncing the name of Mexico City's second largest suburb? Don't! Most locals have shortened it to just **Neza**. Something more chic? **Neza York**. A little more rural? **Mi Nezota**, that is, My Big Neza—a play on words with Minnesota.

Súbanse al coche. Vamos a **Neza York** a los tianguis.

Get in the car. We're going to the street markets in *Ciudad Nezahualcóyotl*.

PUEBLO MÁGICO

LITERAL MEANING: MAGIC TOWN

LOOKING to behold a bunny pulled from a hat? A beautiful damsel sliced in two? A clever card trick? You'll find none of that in Mexico's **pueblos mágicos**. Rather, the country's Tourism Secretariat has bestowed this distinctive label on 121 picturesque towns throughout the country, all as a draw for tourists' money. The real magic? It's a slick marketing trick.

Taxco es uno de los **pueblos mágicos** más conocidos.

Taxco is one of the better known *government-promoted tourist towns*.

3 11

REGIOMONTANO

LITERAL MEANING: ROYAL MOUNTAINEER-LIKE

MMM...What shall we call the residents of our city, Monterrey? We could call them **monterrenos,** but that sounds a bit like **Monte Relleno**, the Stuffed Mountain. Comical, but undignified. Why not switch it around? **Rey=regio** and **Monte=montano**. Easy fix! Reference this regal tag when referring to the residents of Monterrey, Mexico's northern metropolis. For short, just call them **regios**.

> Tras perder su trabajo, un abuelito **regiomontano** de casi 80 años se convirtió en exitoso youtuber gracias a sus recetas de cocina.

> After losing his job, a *Monterrey* grandpa at almost 80 years of age became a successful YouTuber, thanks to his kitchen recipes.

FOREIGN

---

 3 12

GABACHO

LITERAL MEANING: NATIVE TO TOWNS IN THE PYRENEES MOUNTAINS

THOUGH this label was originally coined by Spaniards as a term for the French, Mexicans borrowed and applied it to their neighbors up north.

① Andrés anda con una novia **gabacha**.
Andrés has an *American* girlfriend.

② Siempre compramos los electrónicos en el **Gabacho**.
We always buy our electronics in the *US*.

 3 13

MALINCHISTA

LITERAL MEANING: OF OR REFERRING TO THE WOMAN, MALINCHE

WHO would imagine that the life of an interpreter could bring so much disdain? Just ask Marina (Nahuatl name: **Malinche**), the slave who was sold to conquistador Hernán Cortés and in time became his interpreter and lover. Some scholars attribute much of the Conquest's success to her interpretation

135

skills. Understandably, though, for the Aztecs, she was an enemy, and for some of their descendants today, a traitor. This adjective that bears her name speaks of a love of all things foreign.

Una vez me dijeron **malinchista** por decir que no me gusta el rock en español.

They once called me a *xenophile* just for saying I don't like Spanish rock.

POCHO
LITERAL MEANING: ROTTEN [FRUIT]

LEAVE fruit out for too long and it gets spoiled. Stay out of the country long enough, and the same happens to your Spanish and to your cultural view. That's the premise of the adjective **pocho**.

Andrea fue a California por dos meses y volvió hablando todo **pocho**.

Andrea went to California for two months and came back talking *like an American*.

HISTORICAL

ADELITA
LITERAL MEANING: LITTLE ADELA

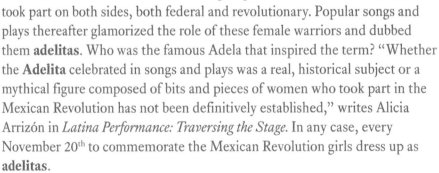

THEY were soldiers in dresses. During the Mexican Revolution from 1910 to 1920, a small group of women took part on both sides, both federal and revolutionary. Popular songs and plays thereafter glamorized the role of these female warriors and dubbed them **adelitas**. Who was the famous Adela that inspired the term? "Whether the **Adelita** celebrated in songs and plays was a real, historical subject or a mythical figure composed of bits and pieces of women who took part in the Mexican Revolution has not been definitively established," writes Alicia Arrizón in *Latina Performance: Traversing the Stage*. In any case, every November 20th to commemorate the Mexican Revolution girls dress up as **adelitas**.

Algunas **adelitas** eran esposas de los soldados.

Some of the *female warriors* were soldier's wives.

BILIMBIQUE

IN a 1913 coup d'état Victoriano Huerta took the reins as president. He ordered that all private banks hand over the precious metals that they held as support for paper currency. Concurrently, he mandated that they emit new bank notes with no such metallic support. The result? The economy tanked. With the public losing faith in such bills, municipalities, military authorities and even businessmen began printing their own bills for use within limited jurisdictions. The downside? They were only valid while the authority who issued them was still in power. One such businessman was William Weeks, who paid his workers in Cananea, Sonora with paper vouchers. By nickname, he was Billy Weeks, and with a Spanish accent **bilimbiques** were born. In response to the COVID-19 pandemic, several municipalities created vouchers that looked like bills as a way to subsidize residents' food purchases at the market. In response, one woman criticized:

Ahora a imprimir **bilimbiques**. Como ya dilapidaron el dinero, hay que inventarlo.

Now let's print some *Monopoly money*. Since they devalued the money, now we have to make up new bills.

Play bank notes can also be called **panchólares**.

NATIONALITIES

CHICANO

IF you were born in the United States but of Mexican descent, what are you? Mexican American or **chicano**? Some feel that the former is an attempt to assimilate them into US culture, while the latter sets them apart. In any case, Mexico's Secretary of Culture posted this:

Recordamos el nacimiento de Ritchie Valens, el primer músico de rock **chicano** que alcanzó la fama en Estados Unidos.

We remember the birth of Richie Valens, the first *American of Mexican descent* who as a rock musician attained fame in the United States.

DIALECTO

WHAT is a dialect? *Merriam-Webster's Dictionary* answers: "A regional variety of language distinguished by features of vocabulary, grammar, and pronunciation from other regional varieties and constituting together with them a single language." A dialect is simply a variation within the same language. There are different dialects of English within the United States, not to mention those from a host of other English-speaking countries. This entire book deals with the Mexican Spanish dialect, which differs from Spanish dialects from elsewhere. Nonetheless, when locals mention a **dialecto**, they refer to one of the country's more than 60 indigenous languages. Is it fair and impartial to call these languages—which are far older than Spanish—mere dialects?

Mi amigo Juan habla el **dialecto** otomí.

My friend Juan speaks the Otomí *language.*

LAS TRES MENTIRAS DEL MEXICANO
LITERAL MEANING: THE MEXICAN'S THREE LIES

WITH a hearty laugh the locals will admit to the three Mexican lies. They are, in no particular order:

① **Está allí nomás.** ① *It's right around the corner.* (Likely miles away.)

② **Lo hago mañana.** ② *I'll do it tomorrow.* (Only symbolically.)

③ **El chile no pica.** ③ *The peppers are not hot.* (Instant gastritis.)

NORTEAMERICANO
LITERAL MEANING: NORTH AMERICAN

IF you are from the US, don't be shocked when Mexicans thus describe you.

Te presento a mi amigo, Bryan. Es **norteamericano**.

I'd like you to meet my friend Bryan. He's *American.*

STATES

¡AY, CHIHUAHUA!

LITERAL MEANING: WOE, CHIHUAHUA!

STUNNED? Surprised? Disappointed? Whatever your strong emotion, let it out with this northern euphemism.

¡Ay, Chihuahua! Ya se acabó el gel antibacterial.

Oh my goodness! The antibacterial gel just ran out.

¡AY, JALISCO, NO TE RAJES!

LITERAL MEANING: JALISCO, DON'T CRACK!

HOW determined are you? Has your mettle been tempered by the fieriest of tests? Popularized by the 1941 Jorge Negrete movie and song of the same name, this injunction is a call to bravery. Muster it up to encourage your troops to never give up, to not permit even the smallest fissure of a crack in their courage. You will frequently hear it as: **¡No te rajes!** It's tantamount to: *Never say die.*

CAMPECHANO

LITERAL MEANING: FROM THE STATE OF CAMPECHE

KINDNESS goes a long way. Just ask the residents of the southern state of Campeche. Their good-natured reputation has spawned this adjective.

   ①   Ese Ródrigo es bien **campechano**. Es muy fácil trabajar con él.

       That Ródrigo is *very kind and easy-going*. He's easy to work with.

Conversely, at the taco stand, remember its alternate meaning: having two or more ingredients.

   ②   Los tacos **campechanos** están a tres por veinte pesos.

       The *mixed* tacos are three for twenty pesos.

CHOCO

LITERAL MEANING: ABBREVIATION OF CHOCOLATE

FROM the Nahuatl *chocolatl*, literally *bitter water*, chocolate originated in Mexico and has spread the world over. Even its abbreviation has gotten fair mileage. Since chocolate is cultivated in Tabasco and some of its inhabitants have dark, chocolaty skin, they've garnered the nickname **chocos**.

El presidente actual de México, Andrés Manuel López Obrador, es **choco**.

Mexico's current president, Andrés Manuel López Obrador, is *from Tabasco*.

HIDROCÁLIDO

EVER been in hot water? The natives of the state of Aguascalientes, that is, Hot Waters, found themselves in that steamy dilemma. What do we call ourselves? According to the *Diccionario de la Real Academia Española*, they officially were dubbed **aguascalentenses**. But that doesn't exactly roll off your tongue; it's hard to pronounce and even harder to remember. Out of practicality, many have opted for this term, a fusion of Greek and Spanish roots. One youngster tweeted:

¡Y yo te mando un saludo **hidrocálido**!

And I send you greetings *from Aguascalientes*!

MEXIQUENSE

LITERAL MEANING: MEXICAN STATER

JUST outside Mexico City you'll find signs for the **Circuito Exterior Mexiquense**, a turnpike that circumnavigates the capital. But why **mexiquense**? Why not **mexicano**? It turns out that **mexiquense** is the adjective to describe residents of the State of Mexico.

Toluca es la capital **mexiquense**.

Toluca is the capital *of the State of Mexico*.

3 | 27

TAPATÍO

LITERAL MEANING: [NAHUATL]
POUCHES OF CACAO BEANS

WHY are Guadalajara's inhabitants called **tapatíos**? One popular theory suggests that during the seventeenth century residents of the nearby town of Tonalá bought and sold with a decadent currency: cacao beans. They placed 10 precious beans in a small bag and then grouped three bags together to form what in Nahuatl was a *tapatiotl*. These simple shoppers were soon called **tapatíos**. On the other hand, **ojos tapatíos** are the almond-shaped eyes typical of the region, while the **jarabe tapatío** is the famed Mexican hat dance.

Mi esposa tiene lindos **ojos tapatíos**.

My wife has beautiful *almond-shaped eyes typical of Guadalajara*.

A GUADALAJARAN SPANISH SAMPLER

Every region has its linguistic idiosyncrasies and Guadalajara is no exception. For your next visit to **Guanatos**, as it's informally called, take this cheat sheet with you.

ÁMOLE	**Ámole** al rancho. → *Let's go* to the ranch.
ARRE	**Arre,** iré mañana. → *OK,* I'll go tomorrow.
BIEN MUCHO	Me gusta **bien mucho**. → I *really, really* like it.
CALADITA	¿Te gustaría una **caladita**? → Would you like *to try* some?
CHARPEADO	Me quedé **charpeado** de aceite. → I was *splattered* with oil.
CHISPEAR	Está **chispeando**. → It's *drizzling*.
EY	¿Quieres ir? **Ey**. → You wanna go? *Yeah.*
LONCHE	Se me antoja un **lonche**. → I feel like eating a *torta* [sandwich].
MELOLENGO	El **melolengo** entró sin tapabocas. → The *idiot* went in without a mask.
SAABE	Te lo dije **saabe**. → I told you so. *Hello!*
TÁMARO	Hoy no he visto a ni un **támaro**. → Today I haven't seen one *transit cop*.

POBLANO

Literal Meaning: a town dweller

EVER heard of the Cinco de Mayo holiday? It commemorates an event that is essentially **poblano**, that is, from the State of Puebla. On May 5, 1862, General Ignacio Zaragoza led undermanned Mexican forces to victory over French troops at the Battle of Puebla. Despite its **poblano** roots, the celebration is far more popular in the United States than in Mexico itself. These days you're more likely to see this term on a menu describing **chiles** or **mole**. One educational site offered the following headline:

Para un buen chile relleno, un buen chile **poblano**

For a good stuffed pepper, get a good pepper *from Puebla*

9

A Little Personality

DEMANDING

3 29

GRILLERO

LITERAL MEANING: CRICKET-LIKE

IT'S night in the bush and you step outside. What do you hear? A symphony? Or a squabble? Odds are that the dominant voices in the fray will be those of the crickets. Do they wait respectfully for their colleagues to finish before chirping anew? Hardly. With all rudeness they butt in and push forward, ranting—oblivious to the cacophony. With good reason, the *Diccionario del español de México* defines the noun **grilla** as: "An atmosphere of murmuring, gossip and slander as produced in political, union, and corporate circles, due to the various attempts of their participants in gaining personal advantage and blocking their rivals." (*Translation ours.*)

Después del accidente en la carretera, tanto el ajustor de seguros como el policía se pusieron bien **grilleros**.

After the accident on the highway, both the insurance adjustor and the policeman became highly *contentious*.

3 30

PONERSE LOS MOÑOS

LITERAL MEANING: TO PUT ON YOUR BOWS

An anxious little girl is getting dressed. It's picture day at school and she wants to look her best. She chooses her favorite dress and puts on her shiniest shoes. The bus will be there in minutes. "Mommie, mommie, my bows! I want bows in my hair!" "There's no time, dear" chides the mother. "No, but I NEED BOWS!" she roars, as she erupts in an epic tantrum. How demanding are you? Offer this idiom in its negative form to convince others that you are a reasonable soul.

Como estoy pidiendo una cita a última hora, no quiero **ponerme los moños**.

Since I am calling for a last-minute appointment, I understand that *beggars can't be choosers.* [Or: *I can't be too picky.*]

`3` `31`

SANGRÓN

LITERAL MEANING: HE WHO BLEEDS A LOT.

IS your friend bleeding? What happened? He has a gusher! In a real emergency, you would call the paramedics. But what if what flows is not blood, but complaints and haughty demands? What if he's hemorraging arrogance? Then you have stumbled upon what Mexicans call a **sangrón**.

① El nuevo novio de mi sobrina es **sangrón**. No lo aguanto.
My niece's new boyfriend is a *pain in the neck*. I can't stand him.

② De volada me doy cuenta cuando alguien está de distante o **sangrón** conmigo.
Right away I realize when someone is distant or *uppity* with me.

IRRITATING

`3` `32`

CANIJO

LITERAL MEANING: SHORT OR SMALL

LOOKING to describe an evil individual, a person who takes advantage of others, someone truly wicked? Look no further than **canijo**.

¡Qué **canijos** mis vecinos! Se metieron a robar mientras anduvimos de vacaciones.

What *scoundrels* my neighbors! They broke in and stole from us while we were on vacation.

`3` `33`

DAR LATA

LITERAL MEANING: TO STRIKE A CAN

REMEMBER *The Gong Show*? It was an '80s talent show with a twist; if a contestant was especially woeful, one of the judges struck a large gong, thus disqualifying them. Beating on a can would be similarly annoying. Pick this idiom for those who likewise grate on your nerves. As an adjective, it's **latoso**.

Marquitos, ¡deja de **dar lata**!

Marquitos, stop *being such a pest*!

DE MALA ONDA
LITERAL MEANING: OF A BAD WAVE

IS it me or are Mexicans frequently talking about frequencies? This bad wave is a grumpy mood, a questionable motive, or something that just stinks.

①   No dormí bien y me levanté **de mala onda**.
    I didn't sleep well and I woke up *in a bad mood*.

②   ¡Qué **mala onda** que por el virus no podemos visitar a los amigos.
    It stinks that because of the virus we can't visit our friends.

③   Cuando la chica entró en la tienda, supe enseguida que era **de mala onda**.
    When the girl came in the store, I knew right away that she had *bad intentions*.

ENCIMOSA
LITERAL MEANING: OF OR RELATED TO BEING ON TOP

SOCIAL distancing is a misnomer. What is needed in a pandemic is *physical* distancing. That's what an **encimosa**, or *clingy* person, can't handle.

Fui al súper y la gente está de **encimosa**; no respeta la distancia.

I went to the supermarket and people are *on top of you*; they don't
   keep their distance.

GORRÓN
LITERAL MEANING: BIG BASEBALL CAP

BEGGARS at times take off their caps and extend them to solicit donations. If you habitually live at another's expense—always letting someone else pay the bill—you will be deemed a **gorrón**.

①   ¿No te da pena llegar de **gorrón**?
    Aren't you ashamed of being a *party crasher*?

②   ¡No seas **gorrón**! También hay que dar.
    Don't be so *selfish*! You also have to give.

3 37

TARUGO
LITERAL MEANING: DOWEL

A DOWEL is a stubby round piece of wood, a device carpenters use to join pieces of wood. How much of an IQ do you think old Woody has? Zilch. That's why the Spanish translation of dowel, **tarugo**, denotes a *dummy*.

¿Viste? ¡Ese **tarugo** trató de invadirme el carril!

Did you see that? That *idiot* tried to come in my lane!

POSITIVE

---

3 38

DE BUENA ONDA
LITERAL MEANING: OF GOOD WAVE

RESTORE your faith in humanity. People with good vibes still exist, as this idiom attests. Some doctors treating COVID patients wrote to colleagues:

①   Les enviamos **toda la buena onda**, que juntos saldremos de esta.
     We send you *our best wishes*; we will make it out of this together.

In contrast, another fellow complained:

②   Qué mal me cae la gente que solo es **buena onda** con los que conocen, y con
     los que no, se hacen los asquerosos.
     I hate it when people are only *nice* to those they know, and with those that they
     don't know, they are disgusting.

3 39

GENTE
LITERAL MEANING: PEOPLE

WITHIN your first week of studying Spanish you learned that **gente** means *people*. What you might not know is that here it's also an adjective.

Mi vecino, Miguel, es bien **gente**.

My neighbor, Miguel, is really *nice*.

3 40

JACARANDOSO

EVERY spring Mexico City streets are bedecked in an explosion of purple flowers, product of the jacaranda tree (*Jacaranda mimosifolia*). A care-free disposition is just as attractive. An article in *El Universal* observed:

Mara Escalante regresa a la pantalla grande interpretando a una mamá **jacarandosa** y exuberante.

Mara Escalante returns to the big screen interpreting a *jovial* and vivacious mom.

3 41

UN PAN DE DIOS

LITERAL MEANING: A BREAD FROM GOD

AS related in the Bible book of Exodus, when the Israelites left Egypt, their menu selections were drastically reduced, the downside to life in the desert. With provisions running out, God miraculously provided manna, a bread from heaven that kept them alive in their wilderness wanderings. Similarly, a person who is there for you in your moment of need could be described as a **pan de Dios**, a real angel.

Ese Jorge es **un pan de Dios**. Durante la pandemia, ni nos nos cobró la renta.

That Jorge is *a real godsend*. During the pandemic, he didn't even charge us rent.

REBELLIOUS/RECKLESS

3 42

AVENTADO

LITERAL MEANING: THROWN

WHAT is thrown aside in this bold adjective is fear. Use it to describe the fearless, the bold—and even the reckless—according to context.

Nunca he sido tan **aventado** como para aventurarme en lo que no he hecho antes.

I've never been *audacious* enough to venture into what I've never done before.

3 43

DARLE VUELO A LA HILACHA
LITERAL MEANING: TO GIVE FLIGHT TO THE HANGING THREAD

OH, the thrill of flying a kite! (See #365, **papalote**.) Once it's airborne, you slowly let the string unwind more and more as your childhood toy reaches ever greater heights. But what if you just let go? The flying polygon and any remaining string will be lost in the wind. Call on this saying to describe what happens when caution is thrown to the wind, and all inhibitions are cast aside. It is the opposite of exercising self-control.

① El borracho **le dio vuelo a la hilacha**; tiene dos semanas que no vuelve a casa.
The drunk *went off the deep end*; he hasn't returned home in two weeks.

② Manuel **le dio vuelo a la hilacha**. Ahora tiene hijos fuera del matrimonio.
Manuel *sowed his wild oats*. Now he has kids out of wedlock.

3 44

REJEGO

FINDING someone under your authority to be uncooperative, unwilling to follow your direction? Then you have discovered a **rejego**. If you have teenagers, you need no further explanation.

Mi chavo es **rejego**; no me hace caso.

My boy is *rebellious*; he doesn't listen to me.

SENSITIVE

3 45

ESTAR SENTIDO
LITERAL MEANING: TO BE FELT

OFFENDED? Then in Mexican Spanish you are **sentido**.

① Camila está **sentida** conmigo porque me burlé de su corte de pelo.
Camila is *mad* at me because I made fun of her haircut.

② Como Roberto no ha llamado a su mamá este mes, ella está **sentida**.
Since Roberto hasn't called his mom this month, she *has hurt feelings*.

JARRITO DE TLAQUEPAQUE

LITERAL MEANING: JUG FROM TLAQUEPAQUE

NOW a part of greater Guadalajara, Tlaquepaque's claim to fame are its works of pottery. Its **jarritos**, or jugs, though beautiful, are fragile. Even the smallest of blows can shatter them. Invoke this image when portraying the thin-skinned and ultra-sensitive.

> Aunque pongas cara de que no pasa nada, por dentro eres un **jarrito de Tlaquepaque**.
>
> Even though you put on that 'Nothing's wrong' face, on the inside you are *super sensitive*.

You may also hear the less common **jarrito de Guadalajara**.

At Your Leisure

MONEY

| 3 | 47 |

AL CHAS CHAS

LITERAL MEANING: [ONOMATOPOEIA]

AS you throw down hard cash on a vendor's table, what noise does it make? The Mexican ear hears this sound. Pull out this phrase to indicate that you are paying in cash.

Si me lo das más barato, te pagaré **al chas chas**.

If you give it to me cheaper, I will pay you *in cash*.

| 3 | 48 |

FERIA

LITERAL MEANING: FAIR

ESPECIALLY in the northern states that border on the US, a store clerk may inquire if you have any of this—*change*. Elsewhere, choose **cambio**.

¿No traes **feria**?

Do you have *change*?

| 3 | 49 |

LANA

LITERAL MEANING: WOOL

TO A shepherd, a sheep's wool was as good as money. The analogy still holds up locally. If a beggar is pestering you for money, just bleat out:

Lo siento, amigo. Ahorita no hay **lana**.

I'm sorry, buddy. Right now I don't have any *money*.

3 50

TANDA

LITERAL MEANING: WORK SHIFT

NEED more self-control to save money? The **tanda** is one solution that leaves banks out of the equation. How does it work? As an example, let's say the coordinator, or **tandero**, collects from ten associates 200 pesos each week. That's a total of 2000 pesos. The first week Associate #1 gets all the money. The next week Associate #2 receives the grand sum, and so forth, until all ten have had a turn at the complete amount. You receive no interest on your money, just peer pressure to set it aside weekly.

¿Quieres entrar a la **tanda** de mi tía?

Do you want in on my aunt's *savings club*?

 3 51

VARO

BACK in the day of the Great American frontier, traders used buckskins to barter. Over time, the shortened form *bucks* became the informal synonym for *dollars*. Similarly, when bargaining, try offering a price in **varos** instead of the formal **pesos**.

Me lo llevo en veinte **varos**. Y te lo doy al chas chas.

I'll give you twenty *pesos* for it. And I'll pay in cash.

MUSIC

 3 52

ANTRO

LITERAL MEANING: CAVERN OR CAVE

DO you have a man cave in your home? Then meet the **antro**. It's a new usage for a term that meant a *cave* in poetic works. Nowadays in Mexico it's a people cave, a nightclub. An *Excélsior* headline read:

En plena pandemia casa se vuelve **antro** en Iztapalapa

In the midst of pandemic a house becomes a *nightclub* in Iztapalapa

ECHARSE UN PALOMAZO

LITERAL MEANING: TO THROW ONESELF A DOVE-STRIKE

JAZZ artists know well that improvisation can sometimes elicit the sweetest of tunes, all in seductive spontaneity. Summon this avian phrase for an impromptu musical session of any kind.

① En la fiesta María y Lucy de repente **se echaron el palomazo**.
At the party María and Lucy suddenly *broke into song*.

② Se le invita a un **palomazo** de jazz.
You are invited to a jazz *jam session*.

PLACES

TIANGUIS

LITERAL MEANING: [NAHUATL] MARKET

IT'S a Saturday morning and you're on the way to grandma's house. Bad idea. Halfway there, you find a thoroughfare clogged with buyers and sellers. It's as if an enormous flea market had spilled into the streets, offering everything from tennis shoes to tacos. Welcome to the **tianguis**, Mexico's famous street markets, which change locations daily. Along the border, refer to them as **sobreruedas**.

Vámonos a chacharear al **tianguis**.

Let's go look around at the *street market*.

TLAPALERÍA

FROM the Nahuatl *tlapalli*, meaning *color*, a **tlapalería** is where you can find a liquid that changes the color of your house—paint. These days **tlapalerías** offer not only paints, but a small selection of other hardware items.

Vete a la **tlapalería** y consígueme un litro de pintura blanca por favor.

Go to the *hardware store* and get me a liter of white paint please.

PURCHASES

3 56

APACHURRADO

MAKE sure that you carefully inspect that papaya you're tempted to buy at the market. Be certain it isn't squashed.

① Mire, señito, esta papaya está toda **apachurrada**. Cámbiemela por favor.
Look, ma'am, this papaya is all *squooshed*. Change it for me please.

② Desde que murió su esposo, Laura ha estado toda **apachurrada**.
Since her husband died, Laura has been completely *depressed*.

3 57

CHAFA

SEPARATING the wheat from the chaff, or hull, has been a farmer's chore since ancient times, today facilitated by automated mills. With a winnowing shovel, the farm hand heaved the cracked wheat into the air, allowing the feathery chaff to be blown away as an unwanted byproduct. There's no evidence that the English *chaff* resulted in the Spanish **chafa.** Even so, the word picture will help you to remember its meaning: *of poor quality*.

No compres ese teléfono; es bien **chafito**.

Don't buy that telephone; it's *garbage*.

3 58

DISPARAR

LITERAL MEANING: TO SHOOT

"DON'T shoot!" How many times have you heard that line—even if from watching too many detective shows? In this particular case, you actually *want* the other person to shoot. Here it means *to pay the bill*.

Muchachos, vámonos a los tacos al pastor. Yo **disparo**.

Hey, guys, let's go out for tacos al pastor. *I'm paying*.

Another option is: **Yo invito**. Up north, choose **Yo picho**.

ENGANCHE

LITERAL MEANING: HOOKING

ARE you hooked? Addicts are. But in this case you are hooking your claim to a property or some other costly purchase. It's the down payment.

¿Cuánto puede usted dar como **enganche**?

How much can you make as a *down payment*?

FORMADO

LITERAL MEANING: TO BE FORMED

IF you learned Spanish in any country not called Mexico, this term is sure to throw you for a loop. I remember waiting in line at a public place when a woman approached and asked: ¿**Está formado**? Since this literally means *Are you formed?*, I first thought to myself: 'Of course, I'm formed of bones and muscle and sinew.' But Mexicans aren't asking about your anatomy.

Disculpe, ¿está **formado**?

Excuse me, are you *in line*?

PILÓN

LITERAL MEANING: A HEAP

HAVE you ever been the recipient of a baker's dozen? You pay for a dozen doughnuts, but the generous baker throws in one more, just because. The **pilón** is a small pylon of raw sugar cane, as pictured here. The kind-hearted seller at the market would often add one of these to the bag as a courtesy. Later, a **pilón** came to mean any freebie.

¿Qué me das de **pilón**?

What will you throw in *for free*?

In southern Mexico, ask for a **ñapa**.

SPORTS

¿ÁGUILA O SOL?

LITERAL MEANING: EAGLE OR SUN?

READY to begin your favorite game? Who starts first? Let's flip for it. To do so, ask your opponent: ¿**Águila o sol**?. That's because on the ten-peso coin an emblematic eagle graces the front while an Aztec sun rock takes front stage on the reverse.

Dilo tú. ¿**Águila o sol**?

You call it. *Heads or tails?*

ALBERCA

LITERAL MEANING: WATER TANK FOR IRRIGATING CROPS

IT'S so hot that the thermometer's mercury is about to burst through the top. Time for a swim! In any other country you might hop into a **piscina**, standard Spanish for *pool*. But not here.

Vámonos a la casa de mis abuelitos. ¡Tienen **alberca**!

Let's go to my grandparents' house. They've got a *pool*!

BOLICHE

LITERAL MEANING: SMALL WOODEN BALL

UP for a game of bowling? Then ask for **boliche**, and not **bolos** as it's known elsewhere. The difference is important because locally a **bolo** is a drunk. Our aim is for the bowling pins to be tipsy, not you.

Mis cuates me invitaron al **boliche** mañana en el centro.

My buddies invited me to go *bowling* with them tomorrow downtown.

PAPALOTE

LITERAL MEANING: [NAHUATL] BUTTERFLY

AS the Nahuatl speaker saw the kite lift ever skyward, what did it remind him of? As it flitted hither and thither, he imagined a hand-fashioned butterfly, a **papalote** in his language.

Salimos con mi hijo a comprar un **papalote**.

We went out with my son to buy a *kite*.

Since a kite has no definite destination, but wanders in the sky above, if someone's life has become a figurative **papalote**, it is without purpose. One woman posted online:

Yo aconsejando a mis amigas cuando mi vida está hecha un **papalote**.

Here I am giving advice to my friends when my own life is *helter-skelter*.

State of Mind

ANGER

A GRITOS Y SOMBRERAZOS

LITERAL MEANING: BY SCREAMS AND HAT SWIPES

THE incensed cowboy yanks off his wide-brimmed hat in a huff. Indignant, he argues with a fellow rancher while in grand gesticulation he brandishes his hat as if it were a machete. Lasso this phrase to describe a loud and scandalous confrontation. It's often the choice to describe over-the-top political ranting.

A gritos y sombrerazos no se arregla nada.

Making a big stink doesn't fix anything.

CORAJE

LITERAL MEANING: COURAGE

WHAT gets under your skin? Unfulfilled promises? Insults? Shoddy merchandise? Whatever the case, in Mexico it will give you **coraje**, or *anger*. Notice that this meaning deviates from standard Spanish, where it denotes *courage*.

Me da mucho **coraje** cuando mis hijos no me hacen caso.

It *makes me mad* when my children don't listen to me.

ECHAR CHISPAS

LITERAL MEANING: TO THROW SPARKS

IT is one thing to be mad and quite another to be infuriated. In this idiom, the rage is such that sparks are flying. Yikes!

Al ver que su niño había roto su vasija favorita, la mamá se puso que **echaba chispas**.

When she saw that her son had broken her favorite vase, the mother was *fit to be tied*.

ESTAR COMO AGUA PARA CHOCOLATE

LITERAL MEANING: TO BE LIKE WATER FOR CHOCOLATE

KNOW how to make hot chocolate? **Step 1:** Bring the water to a boil. **Step 2:** Drop in the chocolate wafer. **Step 3:** Stir. That's not just the recipe for a hot, frothy beverage; it's also a clever way to describe your rage. If you are like water for hot chocolate, then your ire is at the boiling point.

> Ni le hables de su nuevo coche; **está como agua para chocolate** desde que lo robaron.

> Don't even mention his new car; *his blood has been boiling* since it was stolen.

APATHY

ME HACE LO QUE EL VIENTO A JUÁREZ.

LITERAL MEANING: IT DOES THE SAME TO ME AS WHAT THE WIND DID TO JUÁREZ.

BORN in Oaxaca of Zapotec origin, Benito Juárez is a national hero and served as president from 1861–72. How, though, did this impervious-to-the-wind saying come to life? Several theories have surfaced. One is that as a boy he was crossing a lagoon in a small boat with some friends. When strong winds whipped up, his buddies jumped into the water and swam back to shore, while the resolute Benito pressed forward and reached his destination unscathed. To get an idea of the second theory, search online for the 1972 mural of Benito Juárez that Antonio González Orozco painted in Chapultepec Castle. In it Benito stands next to a Mexican flag, which flaps violently in the wind. In the midst of those powerful gusts, Benito doesn't have a hair out of place, much like the plastered coiffures of Hollywood heroes. In a similar vein, many statues of Juárez remain unaffected by the elements. Call on this tough-guy bravado to show your mettle in the face of adversity.

> A: ¿No tienes miedo del virus?
>
> B: **Me hace lo que el viento a Juárez.**

> A: Aren't you afraid of the virus?
>
> B: *I couldn't care less.*

ME VALE GORRO.

LITERAL MEANING: IT'S WORTH HAT TO ME.

EVER lost a hat? Unless there was some sentimentality attached, it wasn't a big loss. This informal phrase expresses as much.

Me vale gorro la política.

I couldn't care less about politics.

NO TE HAGAS COMO QUE LA VIRGEN TE HABLA.

LITERAL MEANING: DON'T ACT AS IF THE VIRGIN WERE SPEAKING TO YOU.

IN Catholic Mexico, claims of virgin sightings abound. But what if someone ignored you because he allegedly was talking with the virgin? That would be a tough argument to swallow. One disgruntled fellow tweeted:

Los responsables ahí son el gobernador corrupto y sus secuaces. **No te hagas como que la Virgen te habla**.

The guilty ones here are the governor and his henchmen. *Don't play dumb.*

PARA TI ESTOY PINTADO.

LITERAL MEANING: FOR YOU I AM PAINTED.

AS part of your home decor, you have carefully hung a large painting of an elegant woman in your dining room. Would you converse with her over lunch? Confide in her? Of course, not; she's nothing more than lines on a canvas. If you receive this complaint, your significant other is feeling likewise neglected. A wife may lament:

Para ti estoy pintada.

I feel like I'm talking to a wall.

See also #210, **pelarle**.

AL PIE DEL CAÑÓN

LITERAL MEANING: AT THE FOOT OF THE CANNON

YOU are in the midst of a war and standing right at the base of the cannon, scanning the horizon for your enemy's next move—on high alert. One daughter-in-law gushed:

> Les deseo a todos una suegra como la mía, siempre **al pie del cañón** conmigo, viendo cada necesidad, consintiéndome y ayudando en todo lo que puede.

> I wish that everyone had a mother-in-law like mine, who's always *attentive* with me, seeing every need, spoiling me and helping all she can.

ABUSADO

LITERAL MEANING: ABUSED

ARE you sharp? Alert at all times? Such persons were called **aguzados** locally, literally *sharpened ones*. In what was likely just a consonant confusion, the term has now been popularized as **abusado**, or **buso** for short.

> Hay muchos ladrones en el mercado. Ponte **buso**.

> There's a lot of thieves at the market. Stay *alert*.

TRUCHA

LITERAL MEANING: TROUT

An article in *Field & Stream* observed regarding this species of fish: "Trout have a blind spot directly behind them, and the closer to the surface they lie, the greater the blind spot. Unfortunately for fishermen, trout seem to be aware of this and compensate for their more limited cone of vision by *heightened wariness.*" (*Italics ours*)

> Cuando vas de compras en Tepito, ponte **trucha**.

> When you go shopping in Tepito, *keep your eyes peeled*.

THE WARY WASP OF THE YUCATÁN

Trout don't have a monopoly on watchfulness. The wasp is equally up to the task. If you're visiting the Yucatán peninsula, convey the same idea as the aforementioned **abusado** and **trucha**, with: **Ponte xux**. In the Mayan language a **xux** (pronounced SHOOSH) is a wasp. Watch out for that!

CONFUSION

CRUDA
LITERAL MEANING: RAW

TOO much to drink? Then you will wake up a bit raw—with a hangover.

Para la **cruda**, tómate un jugo verde.

For a *hangover*, sip on a green drink.

3 78

CUATRAPEARSE
LITERAL MEANING: TO MAKE LIKE A QUADRUPED

IT'S easy enough to get tripped up with two feet. Imagine if you had four! This verb compares our clumsiness to that of four-footed creatures. If you get confused and make a mistake, offer this apology:

①   Lo siento. **Se me cuatrapeó**.
     I'm sorry. *I got all confused.*

②   La espalda **se me cuatrapeó**, pero fui al quiropráctico.
     My back *got messed up*, but I went to the chiropractor.

3 79

DESGARRIATE
LITERAL MEANING: THAT WHICH IS TORN UP

IN Spanish a **garra** is a *claw*, and the verb **desgarrar**, *to tear apart*, as if by a beast. The result of that violent encounter is a mess.

La construcción en la vía ha generado un verdadero **desgarriate**.

Construction on the highway has created real *chaos*.

HACERSE BOLAS

LITERAL MEANING: TO BECOME BALLS

JUGGLERS can handle several balls at a time, with seeming ease. But if you've never done it before, it can be confusing. Let this idiom roll out of your mouth when you're feeling a little mixed up.

> Apenas voy en el Capítulo 2, pero ya **me hice bolas**.

I'm barely in Chapter 2, but I'm already *confused*.

LO BUSCO, LO BUSCO, LO BUSCO, Y NO LO BUSCO.

LITERAL MEANING: I LOOK FOR IT, I LOOK FOR IT, I LOOK FOR IT, BUT I DON'T LOOK FOR IT.

SOME 800,000 Mexicans still speak the Mayan language and countless others have some knowledge of it. Therefore, as odd as the above sentence may sound, for those who were raised in Mayan families, it's completely natural. Why? Because in their language the verbs *to look for* and *to find* are one and the same: *kaxan*. Context indicates to the listener whether the speaker is searching or finding. When Mayans learned Spanish, they simply substituted the Spanish verb **buscar** in each case. In plain English, the above sentence is: *I am looking all over for it, but I can't find it.*

NO CONFUNDAS LA MAGNESIA CON LA GIMNASIA.

LITERAL MEANING: DON'T CONFUSE MAGNESIUM WITH GYMNASIUM.

MAGNESIUM and gymnasium both end with *-ium*. That's where the similarities disappear. One scribe posted:

No confundas la magnesia con la gimnasia; tu analogía no tiene sentido.

Don't mix apples and oranges; your analogy doesn't make sense.

QUEDARSE CON CARA DE WHAT
LITERAL MEANING: TO END UP WITH A FACE OF WHAT

MEXICO'S proximity to the United States makes English encroach further and further upon the native lexicon. The Spanglish in this phrase only accentuates the meaning: to be confused. An embarrassed lady confessed:

> Hoy vi a un chavo parecidísimo a ti y pasé un osote porque le dije: "¿Cómo estás, mi querido?". Y **se quedó con cara de what**.

> Today I saw a guy that looked so much like you that I embarrassed myself big time, because I asked him: "How are you, my dear?". And *he was totally confused*.

SACAR DE ONDA
LITERAL MEANING: TO TAKE SOMEONE OUT OF THE WAVE

PERCHED on a surfboard, you are riding an immense wave when a giant hand snatches you from the action. How would you feel? Angry? Scared? Confused? That's the undercurrent beneath this wave metaphor.

(1) La neta yo sí **me saco de onda** cuando veo a los doctores fumando.
The truth is *it makes me mad* when I see doctors smoking.

(2) Mi maestra me aventó un borrador y a todos **nos sacó de onda**.
My teacher threw an eraser at me and *it freaked all of us out*.

SALIÓ CON SU DOMINGO SIETE.
LITERAL MEANING: HE CAME OUT WITH HIS SUNDAY SEVEN.

HERE'S the fairy tale: A group of dwarves who lived in the forest every night sang the refrain: "**Lunes, martes, miércoles, tres.**" A lumberjack who passed nearby heard their song and suggested that they complete it with: "**Jueves, viernes, sábado, seis.**" That completed the idea and kept the rhyme. Another envious woodsman suggested a final line: "**Domingo, siete.**"

The dwarves who had practiced and perfected their routine were furious; the latest line simply didn't fit. It was completely out of place. Select this saying when a comment is out in left field, or to indicate any egregious error, such as an unwanted pregnancy. A teacher gave these instructions to his class:

① Si va en una ensalada, es una verdura. Si no, es fruta. Y no me vengan con la ensalada de fruta o un **domingo siete**.

If it goes in a salad, it's a vegetable. If not, it's a fruit. And don't come to me with a fruit salad or some other *nonsense*.

② No vayas a salir con un **domingo siete**.

Make sure you don't come home with *a bun in the oven*.

THE THREE FOR EIGHT SPECIAL

Back in the day, at the local pub you could buy small jars of **mezcal** for the bargain-basement price of three pesos. But if you bought three jars' worth, it was even cheaper, just eight pesos. The special was known in Spanish as **tres por ocho**. Those who especially availed themselves of the offer were the town drunks. Inebriated and slurring their words, they began to request a **teporocho**. As a result, to this day **teporocho** is a slang term for a *drunk*.

SE ME CHISPOTEÓ.

THE television series *El Chavo del Ocho* not only left generations in stitches, it also coined phrases that would be forever embedded in the local lingo, including this comical example. Offer this excuse when you speak out of turn.

Disculpe, es que **se me chispoteó**.

I'm sorry. *It just slipped out.*

CRAZINESS

DESCHAVETADO

LITERAL MEANING: DECAPITATED

EVER lost your head? Since the head is humorously referred to as a **chaveta**, if you are **deschavetado**, you've lost it.

En plena pandemia los jóvenes están en fiesta; están **deschavetados**.

In the middle of a pandemic, young people are partying; they've *lost their minds*.

NO LE SUBE EL AGUA AL TINACO.

LITERAL MEANING: THE WATER DOESN'T GO UP TO THE TANK.

THE light's are on, but nobody's home. He has a screw loose. He's one fry short of a Happy Meal. Just as English is filled with lunacy sayings, Mexican Spanish pokes fun at its neighbors by suggesting that the water supply doesn't quite make it to the water tank, usually installed on the house's roof.

> Al hombre **no le sube el agua al tinaco**. ¿Qué puedes esperar de un jugador que tiene aserrín en lugar de neuronas?

> The guy *has lost his marbles*. What can you expect from a player who has sawdust instead of neurons?

PANCHERO

LITERAL MEANING: LIKE PANCHO

WHO was the famous Pancho who gave birth to this popular adjective? José Agustín in his book *La Contracultura en México* suggests two theories. It may allude to the Los Panchos gang, who wreaked havoc in the Mexico City area in the 1970s. Or it may refer to the revolutionary Pancho Villa, whose violent exploits left their mark in history. In either case, **panchero** speaks of the overly dramatic.

① ¡Ay, no seas tan **panchera**!
   My goodness! Don't be *such a drama queen*!

② Se ve que son personas tranquilas que no **arman pancho**.
   It's clear that they are low-key people who don't *make a scene*.

DEPRESSION

ACHICOPALARSE

DOES life have you down? Then Mexicans may describe your state of mind as **achicopalado**, or *discouraged*.

No **se me achicopale**. Verá que encontrará otro empleo.

Don't *get depressed on me*. You'll find another job.

AGÜITARSE

DISCOURAGED? Down in the dumps? Ready to give up? In local lingo, your frame of mind will be characterized as **agüitado**.

No **te agüites**. La próxima vez te van a dar la visa.

Don't be *so sad*. Next time you'll get the visa.

LEFT WHISTLING ON THE HILL

If you have an appointment with someone and get stood up, that's sure to depress you. In said circumstance, you might complain to the no-show: **Me dejaste chiflando solo en la loma**. That literally means: *You left me whistling by myself on the hill*. How dreadful! You might also gripe: **Me dejaste como la novia del rancho**. Translation? *You left me like the ranch bride*. An old wives' tale speaks of a poor country bride who was all dressed up, but left at the altar. If either case, **¡No te agüites!**.

AMOLADO

LITERAL MEANING: PUT TO A GRINDER

HOW does the daily grind affect you? Life's problems may make us feel dejected. This adjective expresses as much.

① Desde que murió su esposo, Noemí anda **amolada**.

Since her husband died, Noemí has been *crushed*.

The related verb **amolar** means *to ruin*.

② ¿Quién **amoló** la microhonda? Ya ni prende.

Who *broke* the microwave? It doesn't even turn on.

If a person acts foolishly or ruins an item, you might chide him with:

③ **Ya ni la amuelas.**

Stop while you're ahead! [The damage is already done.]

DE LA PATADA

LITERAL MEANING: OF THE KICK

HAVE you taken a kick to the gut before? How demoralizing! Kick up this phrase when you are in the sorest of straits.

Desde que perdió su empleo, a Lorenzo le ha ido **de la patada**.

Since he lost his job, Lorenzo has been *in dire straits*.

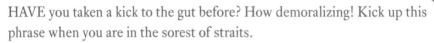

ENCOURAGEMENT

ECHARLE PORRAS

LITERAL MEANING: TO THROW CLUBS

NEED encouragement to stop smoking? To finish a diet? Or just to complete your homework? Why not ask your friends to cheer you on?

Amigas, ya llevo solo siete días en esta dieta. ¡**Échenme porras**!

Girls, I've only been on this diet for seven days. *Cheer me on*!

¡NO TENGAS CUIDADO!

LITERAL MEANING: DON'T HAVE CARE!

THOUGH the literal translation of this phrase makes little sense, here it's employed to mean: *Don't worry!* (Another form is: **No hay cuidado**.) If you accidentally bump into someone, the conversation might go like this:

A: Ah, disculpe.

B: ¡**No tengas cuidado**!

A: Oh, I'm so sorry.

B: *Don't worry about it.*

`3` `96`

¡TRANQUIS!

LITERAL MEANING: BE CALM!

DO you have a companion who tends to get overly excited? Calm him with:

¡**Tranquis**! Todo saldrá bien.

Just chill! Everything will be OK.

FATIGUE

`3` `97`

DESGUANZADO

TIRED? Low on energy? Lethargic? Then offer this explanation:

Hoy me siento **desguanzado**.

Today I feel *exhausted.*

`3` `98`

MOLIDO

LITERAL MEANING: GROUND

THE poor coffee beans have no idea what is about to hit them. They are poured from a bag into the grinder. You put the lid on and hit the button. Their perfectly formed bodies are decimated in a whir of razors that pulverize their defenseless hulls hundreds of times in a matter of seconds. If you were to conduct an exit interview with Señor Bean and ask him how it went, he would surely answer: Estoy **molido**. *I've been through the mill.*

Ya salí de la operación, pero me siento **molido**.

I am out of surgery, but I feel *totally wiped.*

171

FEAR

CHIRIPIORCA

The iconic *Chespirito* television series featured the character known as Chaparrón Bonaparte. Chaparrón was prone to fictitious epileptic-like fits that he called **chiripiorcas**. Though humorous, it can express real anxiety.

El no saber hasta cuándo terminará la cuarentena me está dando la **chiripiorca**.

Not knowing when the lockdown will be over is giving me a *panic attack*.

CURADO DE ESPANTOS
LITERAL MEANING: CURED OF FRIGHTS

IT'S your first day on the job as an emergency room physician, and multi-car accident victims are wheeled in. The blood and guts are overwhelming; you black out and fall with a thud. The next day gunshot-riddled patients beckon your aid. You get a little queasy, but make it through. By the end of the first month, however, even gruesome injuries may become routine. You are now battle-tested, inured to the ghastly trappings of the job.

A: ¿No te da miedo trabajar en urgencias?

B: No, ya estoy **curado de espantos**.

A: Are you afraid to work in the emergency room?

B: No, *nothing surprises me now*.

DARLE COSA
LITERAL MEANING: TO GIVE A THING TO [SOMEONE]

MEXICANS will say it gives them **cosa**, literally a *thing*, as a way of expressing a non-specific emotion, which may be fear, shame, or terror, depending on the context.

① **Me da cosa** borrar las notas porque, ¿qué tal si un día las necesito?
I'm afraid to erase my notes because, what if I need them one day?

② **Me da cosa** comer los chapulines.
Eating grasshoppers *gives me the willies*.

4 02

ÑÁÑARAS

AFRAID or spooked to goosebumps? Then you may have a case of these.

① Las montañas rusas me dan **ñáñaras**.
Roller coasters give me the *heebie-geebies*.

② Siempre que voy al súper me dan **ñáñaras** de sólo ver a las cajeras con los
guantes todos amarillos de lo mugrosos que están.
Every time I go the the supermarket it gives me *the creeps* to see the cashiers
with those gloves that are so filthy they look yellowish.

4 03

NO LE SAQUES.
LITERAL MEANING: DON'T TAKE IT OUT TO [SOMEONE].

FOREIGNERS will find this expression enigmatic. It sounds as if you are
being told to not take out an unspecified something. What locals are
intimating is fear; don't let your fear come out. Don't be a coward.

① **No le saques.** Pídele que sea tu novia.
Don't be a chicken. Ask her to be your girlfriend.

② Sigue aguantando en tu trabajo. **No le saques.**
Keep putting up with your job. *Don't give up.*

PARANOIA

---

4 04

VER MOROS CON TRANCHETES
LITERAL MEANING: TO SEE MAURITANIANS WITH KNIVES

IN Spanish the inhabitants of the North African country of Mauritania are
called **moros**. Since during the Middle Ages Arabs from this region invaded

Spain frequently, the Spanish became paranoid and imagined sightings of knife-brandishing Mauritanians around every corner. Dredge up this saying from ancient history to portray the paranoid.

Si creas que en cada sombra hay un ladrón, estás **viendo moros con tranchetes**.

If you think that in every shadow there's a thief, you're *getting paranoid*.

WILLINGNESS

¡LISTO, CALIXTO!
LITERAL MEANING: READY, CALIXTO!

ARE you ready? Then answer with this childish rhyming phrase.

¡**Listo, Calixto**!

Ready, Freddie!

MÁS PUESTO QUE UN CALCETÍN
LITERAL MEANING: MORE PUT ON THAN A SOCK

HOW ready are you? In this sprightly saying there's a play on words between **puesto** (put) and **dispuesto** (willing). Utter it when you are raring to go.

Ustedes pongan la fecha; yo estoy **más puesto que un calcetín**.

You guys set the date: I'm *an eager beaver*.

SIN QUERER QUERIENDO
LITERAL MEANING: UNINTENTIONALLY WANTING

HERE'S yet another phrase that entered the national consciousness via television, as an utterance of *El Chavo del Ocho*. Though not proper Spanish, it's a tip of the hat to the local culture and may add a sense of humor to your speech—or even get you off the hook.

Quebré la persiana, pero fue **sin querer queriendo**.

I broke the blind, but I *didn't do it on purpose*.

On the Road Again

AIR

ATERRIZAR

LITERAL MEANING: TO LAND

COMING in for a landing? Then you are familiar with this verb. But here you may see it used in new ways.

① Mi jefe solo **aterriza** los días de pago.
My boss only *shows up* on paydays.

② Bien, muchachos, ahora vamos a **aterrizar** las ideas.
OK, boys, now we have *to implement* the ideas.

BOLETO REDONDO

LITERAL MEANING: ROUND TICKET

IN most Latin countries a round-trip ticket is a **boleto de ida y vuelta**. The powerful gravitational pull of the English language up north has skewed the Mexican version to **boleto redondo**.

Dame dos **boletos redondos** para Houston por favor.

Give me two *round-trip tickets* to Houston please.

DARLE EL AVIÓN

LITERAL MEANING: TO GIVE [SOMEONE] THE PLANE

IS someone irritating you? Then tell him to get lost. In local Spanish, I might tell you: **Mándalo a volar**. That literally means: *Send him flying*. What would aid a person to fly and vacate the premises as fast as possible? Why, a plane, of course! If Mexicans give you a figurative plane, they are *ignoring* you. This is especially true if you are dispensing unwanted advice. They may pretend to listen, but secretly they hope that you and the conversation are preparing for an on-time takeoff.

Traté de explicar a mi jefe porque no puedo trabajar los sábados, pero solo **me dio el avión**.

I tried to explain to my boss why I can't work on Saturdays, but he just *ignored me*.

ÍRSELE EL AVIÓN

LITERAL MEANING: TO HAVE THE PLANE LEAVE YOU

WHAT frustration! Your plane has just left without you. At times, it may seem that our thoughts likewise abandon us; they take to flight and leave us mentally back at the gate. Flag down this aviation idiom the next time you lose your train—or plane—of thought.

¿Qué estaba diciendo? **Se me fue el avión**.

What was I saying? *I had a brain fart.*

LAND

AVENTÓN

LITERAL MEANING: A BIG THROW

NEED a ride? In Northern Mexico, ask for a **raite**, Spanglish for *ride*. In the Yucatán, ask for a **botada**. Otherwise, request that your friend kindly throw you to your destination.

Oye, ¿no me puedes dar un **aventón** hasta Avenida La Reforma?

Hey, ¿could you give me a *ride* to La Reforma Avenue?

BANQUETA

LITERAL MEANING: A STOOL

DITCH the generic Spanish **acera** and **andén** and make sure that your feet are firmly planted on the **banqueta**, or *sidewalk*, below you. In the Yucatán, choose **escarpa** instead. See also #117, **cacheteando las banquetas**.

La viejita barre la **banqueta** frente a su casa todos los días.

The old lady sweeps the *sidewalk* in front of her house every day.

4 14

CACHARPO

WHEN traveling on public buses, pay your fare to the **cacharpo,** the assistant who announces stops and helps you with your packages.

Hasta para ser **cacharpo** tienes que saber contar.

Even if you want to be the *bus driver's helper* you have to know how to count.

 4 15

CAJÓN
LITERAL MEANING: BIG BOX

ONE day I received an email at my workplace informing me that I was being assigned a **cajón.** A big box? What kind of a box? It turns out that it's the Mexican Spanish term for *parking space.*

A usted se le ha asignado el **cajón** #65.

You have been assigned *parking space* #65.

 4 16

CAJUELA
LITERAL MEANING: LITTLE BOX

THIS little box is at the rear of your vehicle—the trunk, or boot. Elsewhere in Latin America it's a **baúl** or **maletero.** On the other hand, if you're asked to put something in the **cajuelita,** that's the glove compartment.

Todas las maletas caben bien en la **cajuela.**

All the luggage fits in the *trunk.*

 4 17

CAMELLÓN
LITERAL MEANING: BIG CAMEL

THE median strip is a narrow swath of land that divides two or more lanes of traffic. Imagine that you could slice the entire boulevard and look at it transversally from pavement level. What would you see? The medium strip would appear a large hump in the middle in comparison to the lanes on either side. Some clever wit imagined a large camel and the term has stuck. Lesson? Drive safely—and watch out for those camels.

Tras una discusión con su novia, el joven chocó contra el **camellón**.

After a fight with his girlfriend, the young man crashed into the *median strip*.

THE CHOPPED STREET

Due to the influence of the Mayan language, you will notice many unusual word combinations in the Yucatán peninsula. For example, a local might say that he lives on a **chop calle**. Is that a chopped street? Not exactly. It means a *dead-end street* or *cul-de-sac*, normally expressed in the rest of the country as a **cerrada**.

CAMIÓN

LITERAL MEANING: TRUCK

THROUGHOUT the Spanish-speaking world, a **camión** is a truck. It is in Mexico as well, but here buses are also called **camiones**, which leads to confusion. If you wish to specifically refer to a truck, use **camión de carga**. To reference a tanker truck, choose **pipa**.

Ramón toma el **camión** todos los días para ir a la escuela.

Ramón takes the *bus* every day to go to school.

CHAPOPOTE

MEET the local term for *tar* or *asphalt*. A headline in *ABC Noticias* read:

① Perrita cae a pozo de **chapopote** y es rescatada
Dog falls into a *tar* pit and is rescued.

From an article in *El Universal*:

② La carretera está… perdida entre grandes tramos de terracería y
retazos de **chapopote**.
The highway is…lost between swaths of dirt roads and remnants of *asphalt*.

CHAFIRETE

WHETHER
you're on the bus,
taking a taxi, or even
riding with Uber,
someone has to drive.
What is the driver called? Officially he's a **chofer**. But you will often hear the
more informal **chafirete**. Choose it with discretion, as it may be offensive,
depending on context.

① Manejar una pipa no es trabajo para cualquier **chafirete**.
Driving a tanker truck isn't a job for any old *two-bit driver*.

② Hola, amigo. Parece que voy a ser tu **chafirete** para el domingo.
Hi, buddy. It's looks like you're *stuck with me as a driver* this Sunday.

CLAXON

LITERAL MEANING: BRAND NAME FOR HORNS

SCORE another genericide. Genericide? That's what legal experts call it
when a brand name becomes generic. For example, aspirin began as a brand
name, but its usage became so common that now any pharmaceutical can
produce it and call it *aspirin*. We already saw this happen with #248, **unicel**.
In this case, The Lovell-McConnell Manufacturing Company of Newark,
New Jersey bought the rights to an early horn that made an "awooga" sound,
now associated with antique vehicles. The brand name Klaxon was chosen
from a Greek word that means "I shriek." At least in modern Mexico any
horn is called a **claxon**, a deviation from the standard **bocina**.

En una fiesta de graduación virtual todos se subieron a sus coches y dieron la vuelta
al barrio tocando el **claxon**.

In a virtual graduation party they all got in their cars and started going around the
neighborhood honking their *horns*.

4 22

COFRE

LITERAL MEANING: CHEST OR COFFER

NEED to check your oil? Then pop the hood, that is, the **cofre**. One gentleman boasted on Twitter:

Con el calor aquí en Cancún, acabo de freír unos huevos en el **cofre** del coche.

With the heat here in Cancun, I just fried some eggs on the *hood* of the car.

 4 23

COMBI

LITERAL MEANING: COMBINATION

IN the early '50s Volkswagen introduced its iconic Kombi van. The removable seats made the vehicle versatile; it was a combination that proved massively successful and quickly embraced by the hippie movement. Mexico put the vehicles into service for mass transit. To this day, Mexicans refer to any public minibus, regardless of brand, as a **combi**.

¿Dónde puedo agarrar el **combi** a Indios Verdes?

Where can I catch the *minibus* to Indios Verdes?

 4 24

CONTINGENCIA

LITERAL MEANING: CONTINGENCY

IF you have a Plan A, great! If you also have a Plan B, that's even better. In Mexico City, **contingencia** has acquired a specialized meaning. Surrounded by mountains, the capital suffers from some of the worst air pollution in the hemisphere, in no small part due to the millions of vehicles circulating. To remedy the problem, when the smog becomes intolerable, city officials announce a **contingencia**. Depending on your license plate number, your car may not be able to circulate.

Hoy hay **contingencia**. Hagan planes alternativos de transporte.

Today we are invoking the *emergency plan*. Make alternative transportation plans.

DESBALAGARSE
LITERAL MEANING: TO DISPERSE

IN his book *Así habla el mexicano* Jorge Mejía Prieto explains that this term has its roots in Andalusia, Spain. For the Romani people a **balagar** was a bale of hay. Hence, **desbalagar** came to mean *spreading the straw*. These days it's often employed in its reflexive form; its meaning depends on the context.

1. Durante la cuarentena mi ganado **se desbalagó**.
   During the quarantine my cattle *were scattered about*.

2. Desayuno y ceno según la dieta. Es en la comida donde **me desbalago**.
   I eat breakfast and supper as per my diet. But it's at lunch that I *get off track*.

EN MI RANCHO...
LITERAL MEANING: ON MY RANCH...

REMEMBER the old cowboy movies from the silent film era? A common caption was: "Meanwhile back at the ranch…". Though initially alluding to a literal ranch, the cliché in time transformed into a mere segue between scenes. Likewise today in colloquial speech, Mexicans are prone to preface conversations about the customs of their town with this phrase—even if they grew up in the suburbs.

En mi rancho a las muchachas les decíamos *morras*.

Back home we used to call the girls *morras*.

¿LA LIBRE O LA CUOTA?
LITERAL MEANING: THE FREE OR THE TOLL?

HIGHWAY travel in Mexico can be downright expensive. On certain stretches of road, the toll can be far more than the gas money. Therefore, pay attention when the taxi driver asks you:

¿Quiere que lo lleve por **la libre o la cuota**?

Do you want me to take you *on roads that are free or on toll roads*?

MIS RUMBOS
Literal Meaning: my directions

JOHN Steinbeck once wrote: "We find after years of struggle that we do not take a trip; a trip takes us." Those places that we visit again and again shape who we are. That's what this handy phrase reminds us.

Roma y La Condesa; esos eran **mis rumbos** cuando era chavo.

Roma y La Condesa; those were my *stomping grounds* when I was young.

MUEBLE
Literal Meaning: furniture

OUR Mexican host drove us to a gas station near Piedras Negras, Coahuila where we were going to join another friend of ours. Parking and turning off the motor, the driver turned to me and asked: "¿No sabes qué **mueble** trae?". Since word-for-word that means, Do you know what *furniture* she's coming in?, I was inclined to respond: "I dunno. A love sofa maybe". Lesson? Remember that in northern Mexico any vehicle is a **mueble**.

¿No sabes qué **mueble** trae?

Do you know what *kind of vehicle* she's driving?

NORTEADO
Literal Meaning: pointed north

LOST in the woods? Just look for the North Star to guide yourself to safety. In the Northern Hemisphere, moss usually—but not always—grows on the north side of trees. You would think that this adverb, then, would denote the unwavering and true. In fact, it means the exact opposite: to be lost.

De repente no reconocía nada; me sentí todo **norteado**.

Suddenly I didn't recognize anything; I felt totally *lost*.

4 31

PESERO
LITERAL MEANING: PESO THING

A ride on the bus used to cost a mere peso. As a result, the vehicle itself came to be known as a **pesero**. Since fares have more than doubled, the term is losing popularity, but it's still heard in reference to a **combi**. (See term #423.)

> Antes yo agarraba el **pesero** del trabajo de regreso a la casa.

> Before I used to get a *small bus* from work back to the house.

THE PNEUMONIA-MOBILE

Staying healthy is a priority now more than ever. Who would dare mess with pneumonia? If you visit the lovely port city of Mazatlán, you might think otherwise. There, golf carts have been outfitted as public taxis and are known by the lung-stricken moniker **pulmonías**. But don't fret. When these novelty vehicles began to carry passengers, envious taxi drivers spread the rumor that riding in them would expose you to pneumonia. The false claim was not lost on the public, who have proudly embraced these touristy taxis and their infectious name. Today in Mazatlán there is even a monument to the **pulmonía**.

---

4 32

REFACCIÓN
LITERAL MEANING: SNACK

NEED new brakes? Shock absorbers? A head gasket? Then you are in want of a **refacción**, or auto part, a deviation from the standard **repuesto** or **pieza**. The auto parts store itself is a **refaccionaria**. Note, however, that **refacción** is not limited to car parts; it can refer to any replacement parts for appliances and even electronic equipment. An advertisement prodded:

> ¡Recuerde siempre usar las **refacciones** originales!

> Always remember to use genuine *parts!*

TOPE

LITERAL MEANING: STOPPER

START. Stop. Start. Stop. Start. Stop. Welcome to the maddening Mexican driving experience. Since it seems as if there is a speed bump, or **tope**, every 50 meters, you will wear out your car's clutch—and maybe even your knee joint—in a hurry.

> Mi primo ya arruinó los amortiguadores de su coche porque pasa volando los **topes**.

> My cousin already ruined his car's shock absorbers because he flies over the *speed bumps*.

VOCHO

LITERAL MEANING: BLOCKHEAD

MEXICANS affectionately refer to Volkswagen sedans as **vochos**, or **vochitos**. The word, however, has an etymology that may surprise you. During World Wars I and II French soldiers used *boche* as a slur against Germans, with the approximate meaning of *blockhead* or *idiot*. Since Volkswagens are a German product, its nickname was passed on to the now legendary sedan. Of course, the term has lost any negative connotation in Mexican Spanish, as most locals are unaware of its origin, and have a special place in their hearts for this extraordinary little car. One man pined away on Instagram:

> El **vochito** fue el auto en que aprendieron a manejar nuestros abuelos, nuestros papás, y hasta algunos de nosotros.

> The *Volkswagen sedan* was the car in which our grandparents learned to drive, then our parents, and even some of us.

185

OTHER

EL MUERTO Y EL ARRIMADO A LOS TRES DÍAS APESTAN.

LITERAL MEANING: THE DEAD PERSON AND THE UNINVITED STINK IN THREE DAYS.

AS you travel, be careful not to overstay your welcome. Benjamin Franklin, by way of John Lyly, gave us "Fish and friends stink in three days." In this Mexican version, a cadaver and an **arrimado**, that is, an uninvited visitor, will turn up your nose. Why not bring up this saying on the third day of your visit to gauge your host's willingness to extend your stay?

HECHO LA MOCHA

LITERAL MEANING: MADE THE CUT-OFF THING

DURING railroad's heyday, a practical need arose in the rail yards in order to service the trains. The large locomotives had a difficult time maneuvering the narrow spaces. The solution? Smaller engines were brought in. These units garnered the nickname **mocha**, from the verb **mochar**, *to cut off* or *shorten* because, compared to the full-size engines, they appeared clipped. These little guys were not only more agile, they gave birth to this swift idiom.

> Cuando a mi abuelo le dio el infarto, mis papás y yo tuvimos que irnos **hechos la mocha**.

> When my grandpa had a heart attack, my parents and I had *to high-tail it* out of here.

WATER

TRAJINERA

DON'T leave Mexico City without visiting Xochimilco and taking a ride on a **trajinera**, the colorful wooden boats that tour you around the canals.

> Es muy relajante dar un paseo por los canales en **trajinera**.

> It's very relaxing to take a tour on the canals in a *typical wooden boat.*

All in a Day's Work

ABILITY

4 38

AGUANTAR UN PIANO
LITERAL MEANING: TO ENDURE A PIANO

HOW much can you handle? A fellow who casually throws a piano on his back and strolls away with it would have to be especially stout. Pick up this strongman hyperbole to extol the exceptional.

① La actriz tiene más de 50 años pero todavía **aguanta un piano**.
The actress is more than 50 years old, but she still *looks fantastic*.

② Asahel es un albañil que **aguanta un piano**.
Asahel is an *excellent* bricklayer.

4 39

ATORÁRSELE LA CARRETA
LITERAL MEANING: TO HAVE THE CART GET STUCK

YOU are guiding the oxen that pull a cart of hay back to the barn. Before arriving, the cart gets stuck. Are you capable enough to dislodge it and get going? This barnyard metaphor speaks of anyone having a hard time of it.

① Cuando a los jóvenes **se les atora la carreta**, prestan dinero de sus papás.
When young people *get in a bind*, they borrow money from their parents.

② A Juan **no se le atora la carrreta**.
Juan *always finds a way to get the job done*.

4 40

CHIPOCLUDO

CARTOONIST Gabriel Vargas created the *Familia Burrón* comic strip, which ran from 1948 to 2009. Since **burrón** equates to *stupid*, a loose translation might be *The Dimwits*. Superbly creative, Vargas incorporated Mexican Spanish in his work and even coined the term **chipocludo**.

Enrique es el electricista más **chipocludo** que conozco.

Enrique is the most *qualified* electrician I know.

4 41

DAR EL ANCHO
LITERAL MEANING: TO GIVE THE WIDTH

WE may have to search far and wide to find something of good quality. The width, or **ancho,** mentioned here reminds us we must measure up to certain standards—or else.

Probaron a Julio como cajero en el banco, pero no **dio el ancho**.

They tried Julio as a bank teller, but he *didn't make the grade*.

4 42

EL QUE NACE PARA TAMAL, DEL CIELO CAEN LAS HOJAS.
LITERAL MEANING: FOR THE ONE BORN [TO BE A] TAMALE, THE HUSKS FALL FROM HEAVEN.

WERE you born to sing? To dance? To excel in some sport? Some people arrive on Planet Earth with certain innate talents; it's as if the stars had aligned to carry them to success. In this culinary saying, if you were born to be a tamale, the corn husk wrappings would drip from the heavens. *You were born for this.* Others, conversely, apply the adage in a negative light. If you are not skilled at a given activity and this saying is uttered, it implies: *You weren't meant for this*. In either case, it suggests that destiny has played a role in your current state of affairs.

 4 43

FREGÓN
LITERAL MEANING: BIG BOTHERER

DO you like to tease others? Then you may be scolded with: **No friegues**. *Don't bother me.* The especially gifted bother us just because we don't measure up to their brilliance.

Mi médico es tan **fregón** que, con solo verme, me recupero.

My doctor is so *skilled* that, just looking at me, I get better.

NO CANTA TAN MAL LAS RANCHERAS.

LITERAL MEANING: HE OR SHE DOESN'T SING THE RANCH SONGS SO POORLY.

IF this slightly sarcastic saying is applied to you, it's not exactly a ringing endorsement, but neither is it a condemnation.

¿No has pensado en noviar con María? **No canta tan mal las rancheras**.

Haven't you considered dating María? *She's not so bad after all.* [Or: *She might actually be a good option.*]

NO ME SALE.

LITERAL MEANING: IT DOESN'T LEAVE ME.

YOU have studied the manual over and over again. You've asked fellow employees for pointers to get it right. You practice *ad nauseum*. And yet, performing the assigned job eludes you. In defeat, you admit:

No me sale.

I can't get the hang of it.

NO, MIS RESPETOS.

LITERAL MEANING: NO, MY RESPECTS.

IMPRESSED by a worker's skill? His endurance in a thankless job without fanfare? By some altruistic act? If so, tip your hat with this pithy phrase.

① El señor Rodríguez ha aguantado en este trabajo por 50 años.
   No, mis respetos.
   Mr. Rodríguez has endured in this job for 50 years. *You've got to admire him.*

② ¡Qué increíbles las enfermeras en esta pandemia! **No, mis respetos**.
   The nurses have been incredible in this pandemic. *We salute them.*

TENER CALLO

LITERAL MEANING: TO HAVE CALLUS

HARD physical work leaves its mark on our hands. We develop calluses, preparing us to cope ever better with the workload. What other machine adapts so well to the task? In the same way, life experience can harden us to certain unpleasantries. One woman posted:

Tengo callo en las decepciones y la resignación.

I have experience with disappointment and accepting adversity.

TENER COLMILLO

LITERAL MEANING: TO HAVE FANG

AS we age, our gum line gradually recedes, revealing more of our our canine teeth, each of which is called a **colmillo**, literally a *fang*, in Spanish. Does this explain why this idiom means to be wise or experienced? You may also describe such a person as **colmilludo**.

A Pedro no se lo engañan fácilmente. **Tiene colmillo**.

Pedro is not easily fooled. *He's as sharp as a tack.*

A la hora de comprar un vehículo hay que ser **colmilludo**.

When buying a vehicle, you must be *savvy*.

AUTHORITY

ACHICHINCLE

LITERAL MEANING: [NAHUATL] THE ONE WHO SUCKS WATER

IN many sports the water boy has a simple job: to have drinks on hand and keep the athletes hydrated. The **achichincle** is the Mexican version of the water boy—minus the athletics. Originally, these mine workers carried buckets of water from subterranean springs. In time, it came to mean a lowly helper or servile flatterer. One woman wrote of her first job:

Mi primer trabajo fue en Segob, **achichincle** del **achichincle** del **achichincle**.

My first job was in the Segob [Mexican Secretariat for Home Affairs], *helper* of the *helper* of the *helper*.

AMACHINARSE
Literal Meaning: to marry out of wedlock

DESPITE its literal meaning, locals emphasize the macho aspect of the verb. Now it means *to arbitrarily take something* or *to be a tough guy*.

① **Se amachinó** el frío en México. Espero no amanecer congelado como mamut.
The cold *took over* in Mexico. I hope not to awake frozen like a mammoth.

② Su mamá le pellizcó al niño, quien **se amachinó** y no lloró.
His mom pinched the boy, but he *made like a tough guy* and didn't cry.

BAJARLE LOS HUMOS
Literal Meaning: to lower the smokes

IF arrogance were smoke, the conceited one's face would be enshrouded in smog. This popular phrase suggests taking action to burst the bubble of hubris that engulfs the snob.

Ahora Pepe se cree demasiado. Hay que **bajarle los humos**.

Lately Pepe thinks too much of himself. *He must be brought back to Earth.*

EL MERO MERO
Literal Meaning: the very very

MEXICANS employ **mero** as an intensifier. "La **mera** verdad" means the *real* truth. But here the repeated adjective becomes a noun: the one with maximum authority. When you enter a room, walk up to someone and ask:

¿Es usted **el mero mero**?

Are you the *one in charge*?

4 53

ENTRA COMO PEDRO POR SU CASA.

LITERAL MEANING: HE ENTERS LIKE PEDRO IN HIS HOUSE.

YOUR landlord waltzes through the door of the house, opens your refrigerator, helps himself to a beer, and swigs it down. How would you feel? Indignant! This popular saying paints just such an audacious intruder as a nondescript Pedro, or sometimes a Juan, as seen below.

> Vamos a seguir quedándonos en nuestra casa, mientras la gente que llega del exterior **entra como Juan en su casa** al país.
>
> We are going to keep staying at home, while people that come from abroad just *come waltzing right into* the country *like they own the place.*

 4 54

PINTA TU RAYA.

LITERAL MEANING: PAINT YOUR LINE.

DRAWING a line in the sand is not art; it's a statement of authority. If a workmate takes undue liberties, this line will put him in his place.

> **Pinta tu raya**.
>
> *Back off.* [Or possibly: *Know your place.*]

 4 55

PONERSE AL TÚ POR TÚ

LITERAL MEANING: TO PUT YOURSELF YOU FOR YOU

WANT to show respect to an older person or a stranger? Then address them with the pronoun **usted;** reserve the more informal **tú** for close friends or children. In putting oneself at the same pronoun level, as suggested in this phrase, you are either brave or are disrespecting authority.

① La Guardia Nacional espera **ponerse al tú por tú** con el crimen organizado.
The National Guard hopes to be *up to par with* organized crime.

② El chavo **se puso al tú por tú** con su jefe.
The young man *stood up to* his boss.

COMPLETION

DARLE MATARILE

LITERAL MEANING: TO GIVE DEATH TO

BOYS and girls frolic in the street. Spontaneously all join hands in a circle as they dance and sing: "Amo a to, **matarile** rile rón." Today, the lyrics are little more than playful gibberish. Where did they come from? Surprisingly, they originated as French lyrics of a child's song which started with the words: "Ah! Mon beau château!" (Oh, my beautiful castle!). Youngsters from Spain who heard the song in French sang it as they perceived it in their language. Other deformations happened as it spread through Mexico and elsewhere, leaving the lyrics unrecognizable. Since **matarile** sounds like an extension of the verb **matar**, *to kill*, it entered the language with that dark meaning. These days it's often used in a more symbolic way, as these examples illustrate.

① Después de cocinar el pozole, a **darle matarile** a la olla.
   After you cook the pozole, you've got *to finish off* the pot.

② Siempre usamos las mismas mentiras para **darle matarile** a una relación.
   We always use the same lies *to put an end* to a relationship.

O JALAS O TE PANDEAS.

LITERAL MEANING: YOU EITHER PULL OR YOU SAG.

HOW committed are you? This phrase begs the same question. **Jalar** in its primary sense means *to pull*. Figuratively, if you help someone else to pull, you are *supporting* them or *accompanying* them. In other contexts, it means *to work*, a synonym of **chambear**. In contrast, **pandearse** means *to sag*. For example, Latins will use this verb when ceiling tiles start to buckle, perhaps due to moisture. Symbolically, if a person rejects your offer, they are sagging, or drawing away from you. To illustrate, your friend invites you to become his new business partner. After describing his proposal, he asks pointedly:

¿**O jalas o te pandeas**?

Are you with me or not?

DIFFICULTY

LA HORA DE LA HORA
LITERAL MEANING: THE HOUR OF THE HOUR

YOUR team is losing 3-2. It's the bottom of the ninth and there are two outs as you step to the plate. The bases are loaded, but the pitcher works the count to three balls and two strikes. The pitcher winds up, throws, and—. Do you know what time is it? It's the most decisive moment of the ballgame. It's what Mexicans would call **la hora de la hora** or **la mera hora**.

A la hora de la hora, Pérez se ponchó y su equipo perdió.

When *the moment of truth* came, Pérez struck out and his team lost.

NO ES CUESTIÓN DE 'ENCHÍLAME OTRA.'
LITERAL MEANING: IT'S NOT A QUESTION OF 'DIP ANOTHER TORTILLA IN THE SAUCE.'

EVER made enchiladas? The most time-consuming task is preparing the meat you select. And the easiest step is taking a tortilla and dipping it in the spicy sauce, just before you put your meat inside and roll it up. Pick this spicy saying when you need to explain to someone: *It's not as easy as you think.*

TALACHA

FROM the Nahuatl *tlalli*, earth, and the Spanish **hacha**, or axe, a **talacha** refers to any instrument used to work the earth, such as a hoe. That's definitely a  job that will get your hands dirty. For that reason, today it's a buzzword for any difficult job. Many roadside stands that offer to fix damaged tires have a simple sign that reads: **TALACHA**.

No vayas a meter todos los datos a la compu a mano. Es una **talacha**.

Don't think about entering all the data in the computer by hand. That's a *dirty job*.

TRAER EL NIÑO ATRAVESADO

LITERAL MEANING: TO BRING THE BOY CROSSWAYS

THE first birth pangs have started. Excited and worried, the pregnant mother rushes to the hospital, only to be informed by the attending physician that there's a big problem. The baby is not head down, as should be the case, but is sideways, or transverse. Yikes! Call on this pregnancy parallelism when an ugly problem has reared his head. One woman whined:

> Es domingo a las seis de la tarde y estoy en la oficina **con el niño atravesado**, sin Internet y se acaba de ir la luz.

> It's Sunday at six in the afternoon, I am at the office, and *Houston, we have a problem*. There's no Internet and the electricity just went out.

EFFORT

ECHARLE LOS KILOS

LITERAL MEANING: TO THROW ON THE KILOS

AT the market, even tortillas are sold in kilos. To set up shop, a worker may have to carry and move many kilos. Lift this heavy idiom when you are giving your maximum effort.

> Estamos **echándole los kilos** para terminar la casa nueva lo más pronto posible.

> We *are giving it our all* in order to finish the new house as soon as possible.

ENGUASADO

BUSY? Stressed? In the western state of Nayarit, just explain that you are **enguasado**, sometimes spelled **enhuasado**.

> No lo puedo atender ahorita. Ando bien **enguasado**.

> I don't have time for you right now. I'm very *busy*.

SUDAR LA GOTA GORDA

LITERAL MEANING: TO SWEAT THE FAT DROP

IF you are barely breaking a sweat, each droplet of perspiration will hardly be noticeable. In contrast, bloated spheres of liquid waste will drench the engaged worker in short order.

> Yo trabajo en el mercado de sol a sol **sudando la gota gorda**.
>
> I am in the market from dawn to dusk *working my tail off.*

GENERAL

BOMBERAZO

LITERAL MEANING: FIREMAN SWIPE

THE telephone rings at the firehouse. There's a five-alarm fire raging at a public school. Will the dispatcher nonchalantly respond: "Let's see if we can schedule something for tomorrow"? Of course not! It's urgent! Dial up this firefighter analogy for any urgent job that arises.

(1) Juan, tenemos un **bomberazo**. ¿Puedes venir a la oficina temprano hoy?
Juan, we have an *urgent job*. Can you come to the office early today?

(2) Fue un torneo que literalmente se organizó **de bomberazo**.
It was a tournament that literally was organized *at the last minute.*

CHAMBA

LITERAL MEANING: BY CHANCE

BE grateful if you have a **chamba**, Mexico's word for *work*. Notice how its form and meaning change when converted into an adjective.

(1) Voy para la **chamba**.
I am headed to *work*.

(2) Carlos es bien **chambeador**.
Carlos is very *hard-working*.

CHANGARRO

ACCORDING to the colloquial dictionary *Chilangonario* this term came from the now archaic **zangarro**, a shack where illegal booze was dispensed. It specifically refers to small stores, perhaps in a booth or at a stand.

①   Voy a poner un **changarro** de accesorios de celulares.
    I am going to set up a *kiosk* to sell mobile phone accessories.

If you are the one in charge of your work area, you might informally tell your assistant before stepping out:

②   Cuídame el **changarro**; ahorita regreso.
    Watch over the *business* for me. I'll be right back.

DE PLANTA

LITERAL MEANING: OF PLANT

TRANSPLANTING even a daisy has its risks. Will it respond well to the new soil? Will it have enough sunlight or too much? How about the irrigation? If even plants suffer when uprooted, how much more so workers who jump from one corporation to another. For those who make the adaptation well, there is good news: the bosses may view them as well-planted, permanent members of the company. In this phrase **planta** is likely a shortened version of **plantilla**, the payroll, where such permanent workers' names are listed.

Ricardo es contador **de planta** en nuestra empresa.

Ricardo is an *in-house* accountant for our company.

ILLEGAL

CACHIRUL

SOCCER is the unquestioned king in Mexico. In 1988, however, a scandal tarnished the country's participation in the CONCACAF Under-20 tournament. It was discovered that four players on the Mexican national team were in fact over 20 years of age. Since **cachirul** was already a slang term for an illegitimate child or a cheat of any kind, the entire team was given the dubious nickname **los cachirules**, and the scandal itself, **el cachirulazo**. Since then the term is often applied to anything fake.

Se me hace que el doctor de la esquina es un médico **cachirul**.

I have the impression that the doctor on the corner is a *fake*.

FAYUCA

IS that Prada purse real? What about that Rolex watch? Watch out! It could be contraband.

En Tepito se vende todo tipo de **fayuca**.

In Tepito all sorts of *pirated goods* are sold.

HUACHICOLERO

AS one of the world's leading oil producers, Mexico has its share of pipelines. However, bands of organized crime tap into the lines, syphon off the gas, and sell it illegally. These fuel thieves are known as **huachicoleros**. One headline announced:

Cae **huachicolero** con 30 galones de diésel

Fuel thief caught with 30 gallons of diesel

INFORMAL

FRANELERO

LITERAL MEANING: RAG PERSON

AT a red light in Mexico, your car stops, but the show barely begins. Jugglers on unicycles, clowns and others emerge on the crowded crosswalk stage. Human dragons take a swig of gasoline and launch tongues of fire into the acrid air, already saturated with carbon monoxide. A bevy of forlorn youngsters sprint to squirt soapy water on the windows and wipe them off with half-amputated squeegees before the light turns. A parade of itinerant salespeople hawking everything from energy drinks to tamales stream past you. And then there's the **franelero**. Since a cleaning rag here is called a **franela,** the **franelero** is the one who with said rag starts wiping the dust off your hood in a whirl and, given enough time, will "clean" your car's entire chassis. Yes, the complete circus is in full swing, all for a few-pesos tip.

¡Qué coraje! El **franelero** se acaba de rayar la pintura del coche.

I am so mad! The *guy with the rag* just scratched the car's paint.

HUESEAR

LITERAL MEANING: TO BONE

THERE'S a reason they're called *starving* artists. Making a steady living in the entertainment industry is the privilege of a select few. If you can't have the whole pork chop, why not nibble on the bone? That's the idea here. **Huesear** encompasses accepting sporadic gigs or even other work not related to the applicant's talents.

Algunos egresados del Instituto de Música se la pasan **hueseando.**

Some Music Institute graduates *work in any job that comes their way.*

PEPENADOR

LITERAL MEANING: [NAHUATL] ONE WHO CHOOSES OR SELECTS

YOU would expect the garbage dump to be a quiet final resting place for the refuse that lands there. But you would be wrong. The dumps are teeming with **pepenadores.** Youngsters slice through bags, searching for metal, for plastic, for anything that can be sold. Old men wield dollies swollen with cardboard through busy streets. Out of the muck determined women take the reins of emaciated horses who pull battered carts loaded with the day's finds. In the stench and in the face of unspeakable danger, these reticent recyclers trudge forward. They did not choose this job; it chose them.

Los **pepenadores** sobreviven de lo que logran rescatar de la basura.

The *indigent trash recyclers* survive from what they can salvage from the garbage.

VIENEVIENE
LITERAL MEANING: COME COME

DID you actually think you were capable of parking your car at the grocery store by yourself? Think again! As soon as you pull into the lot, a parking attendant will come running to your rescue. After a few toots of the whistle, they will cry out: "**Viene-viene, viene-viene**." When you have reached an adequate distance between your vehicle and the next, a hand gesture or additional whistle toot will signal the end of the ride. Congratulations! You have parked your car! Tip, please.

Mi tía está trabajando de **vieneviene** en el súper.

My aunt is working as *an informal parking attendant* at the supermarket.

TIPS TO THE TIPPING POINT

Consider that many **vieneviene** work in lots that *already* charge parking fees. Their tip money is a fee upon a fee. Their work overlaps that of the **franeleros** mentioned in term #472. That's because they may have their own rag and offer to dust off your car in addition to help you park it. **Franeleros** have also taken over certain sections of public streets and will charge people to park and watch their vehicles. Their acting as if they own the streets has driven some local residents to the tipping point.

OUT OF ORDER

DESCONCHINFLADO
LITERAL MEANING: DETERIORATED

IT'S five o'clock on Friday and you have just finished an urgent report. You hit the print button at your computer and head to the printer. But when you arrive, your heart sinks; a workmate has left a hand-written sign that reads: **DESCONCHINFLADO**. The printer is *out of order*. Sigh. Dust off this depressing descriptor when what should be working isn't.

No puedo creer que la impresora todavía siga **desconchinflada**.

I can't believe that the printer is still *broken*.

PAPERWORK

---

4 77

ENMICAR

NEED to laminate a document? Then pick this verb, which differs from the standard **plastificar** or **laminar** used elsewhere. Mexicans may also refer to their American visa as a **mica**, since it is often laminated within the passport.

¿Cuánto me costaría **enmicar** esta hoja?

How much would it cost *to laminate* this sheet?

4 78

PLUMÓN

LITERAL MEANING: BIG FEATHER

READY for the highlight of your day? Look no further. In much of Latin America a **pluma** is a pen. But this enlarged version, **plumón**, refers to a *highlighter*.

Con un **plumón** marca la respuesta en cada párrafo.

With a *highlighter* mark the answer in each paragraph.

RECIPROCITY

---

4 79

ARRIEROS SOMOS Y EN EL CAMINO ANDAMOS.

LITERAL MEANING: WE ARE CATTLE DRIVERS AND WE WALK IN THE WAY.

FROM dawn to dusk, the cattle driver was usually somewhere on the road, moving animals and other goods from one place to another. What if while on the run a problem should arise? It's not as if they could call the local automobile association or the insurance company to lend a hand. That's why they would rely on their fellow ranchers, the other **arrieros**. The implication is that if your fellow rancher is in need, you better help him. Because the next time you might be the one in need of aid. Consider this saying a fair translation of: *What goes around, comes around.*

4 80

QUÉ LA VOLUNTAD DE DIOS SE HAGA EN LOS BUEYES DE MI COMPADRE.

LITERAL MEANING: MAY THE WILL OF GOD BE DONE IN MY SON'S GODFATHER'S OXEN.

DO you play by the rules? Or do you expect everyone else to do so while you flaunt the law? How do you feel when your doctor tells you not to smoke, but he smells like a chimney? Or when the policeman on a motorcycle gives you a ticket even though he's not wearing a helmet? Surely such hypocrisy makes you indignant. In this saying the will of God represents the law, and instead of following it yourself, you are expecting only your buddy and others to toe the line. The brazen one who utters this saying in effect is declaring: *I live by my own rules.*

SOLIDARITY

---

 4 81

COOPERACHA

LITERAL MEANING: [DISTORTION OF] COOPERATION

HAS a colleague fallen on hard times and needs help to pay a medical bill? Then pull resources with a **cooperacha**, an informal fund for the needy.

> Organizaron una **cooperacha** para ayudarle a Mario cuando perdió el empleo.

> They organized a *fund among themselves* to help Mario when he lost his job.

TRADES

---

4 82

GUARURA

LITERAL MEANING: [TARAHUMARA] BIG, IMPORTANT

IN this violent world, the self-proclaimed important ones—whether politicians, movie stars, or drug lords—need protection. Enter the **guarura**, the bodyguard, a hand-down from Tarahumara, still spoken in Chihuahua.

> El **guarura** del alcalde mató al asaltante.

> The mayor's *bodyguard* killed the assailant.

HOJALATERO

LITERAL MEANING: BUYER OR SELLER OF METAL SHEETING

DID you just get into an automobile accident? If the car wasn't totaled, it could be worth fixing. Just look for a trustworthy **hojaletero**, or auto body technician, many of whom work out of their own homes.

Javier fue mi **hojalatero**; me arregló un coche chocado que había comprado.

Javier was my *auto body guy*; he fixed a damaged car I had purchased.

JIMADOR

LITERAL MEANING: SCRAPER OR CUTTER

THE blue agave plant hides its treasure directly beneath it. What appears to be an enormous pineapple is the prime material for tequila. But to prepare these pineapples for the distillery is no small task. Enter the **jimador**, as seen here. The verb **jimar** means *to scrape* or *to cut*. The instrument seen here, similar to a hoe but with one straight blade, is a **jimador**, or *scraper*. And the worker himself has come to be called by the name of his implement. To muddy the semantic waters even more, since **El Jimador** is also a major brand name for tequila, some use it as a synonym for the drink itself.

Si no fuera por el trabajo arduo del **jimador**, no tendríamos nada de tequila.

If it weren't for the back-breaking work of the *agave scrapers*, we wouldn't have any tequila.

MARIACHI

LITERAL MEANING: [FRENCH] MARRIAGE

THERE is strong suspicion that the term **mariachi**, a staple of Mexican culture, was in fact borrowed from the French. From 1864–67 Maximilian ruled over the country. During that time some say that French soldiers would invite the local bands to play at their weddings, the commencement of a *mariage*. Try this: Search for "Translate wedding English to French" on Google and click the sound icon of *mariage* [the French translation] to hear a native speaker pronounce it. The similarity between it and **mariachi** is uncanny. Yes, **mariachi** has a certain *je ne sais quoi* about it.

El abuelo pagó para que los **mariachis** tocaran en la boda de su nieta.

The grandfather paid for *a Mexican band of trumpeters, guitarists, and violinists* to play at his granddaughter's wedding.

PROFESIONISTA

LITERAL MEANING: PROFESSIONAL

DO you have a college degree? Then Mexicans will refer to you as a **profesionista**, especially if you are practicing your studied profession.

Es una lástima que haya tantos **profesionistas** sin trabajo.

It is a shame that there are so many *college graduates* without a job.

TRAILERO

LITERAL MEANING: TRAILER MAN

THOUGH trucks in general are called **camiones**, semis pull a trailer, which locals have adapted from English as **traila**. The driver, of course, is a **trailero**.

Ese restaurante siempre está lleno de **traileros**.

The restaurant is always filled with *truck drivers*.

VELADOR

LITERAL MEANING: ONE WHO STAYS UP AT NIGHT

KEEP on the watch! That's quite a chore at 3 a.m. In any case, that's the assignment for the **velador,** or night watchman, known elsewhere as a **vigilante** or **guardia nocturna**. See also #79, **tecolote**.

El trabajo de **velador** es agotador.

Night watchman work is exhausting.

UNORTHODOX

A LA BRAVA

LITERAL MEANING: BRAVE STYLE

WALKING on the correct side of the line that separates bravery and recklessness is not always easy. This phrase generally falls to the latter category.

① El chofer estaba manejando **a la brava** y chocó contra un poste de luz.
The driver was driving *recklessly* and slammed into an electrical pole.

② Los vendedores erigieron puestos en la banqueta **a la brava**.
The sellers set up stands on the sidewalks *without permission*.

A LA VIVA MÉXICO

LITERAL MEANING: LONG LIVE MEXICO STYLE

A Mexican friend and I were standing at the corner of a very busy intersection trying to cross the street. Since so many drivers regarded the red light as a mere suggestion, we were having a hard time getting to the other side. Bewildered, I looked at him and asked: "How are we ever going to get across?". Never will I forget his response:

¡Vamos **a la viva México**!

Let's *wing it*!

4 91

AL AHÍ SE VA
LITERAL MEANING: IT'S ON ITS WAY STYLE

THERE is a rush order that has been hastily put together. No one has verified the details of the request, and no one has checked the quality. Instead, speed has been the primary consideration. As soon as the shipping label is printed, the company tells the customer: **Ahí se va**. *It's on its way!* Call on this phrase when work is performed shoddily.

① Si tomas las decisiones **al ahí se va**, llegarás a la ruina.
If you make *haphazard* decisions, you will come to ruin.

② Construyeron ese puente **al ahí se va**; en menos de un año ya tiene fisuras.
They built that bridge *helter skelter*; in less than a year it has cracks in it.

UTENSILS

 4 92

CERILLO
LITERAL MEANING: WAX CANDLE

YOU will need this little stick to light the candle: a *match*. It's also the term for the person who packs your bags at the grocery store.

Fui al supermercado para comprar unos **cerillos**; luego tuve que darle una propina al **cerillo**.

I went to the supermarket to buy *matches*; then I had to give a tip to *the guy who packed my bags*.

 4 93

DIABLITO
LITERAL MEANING: LITTLE DEVIL

DO you see two handles or two horns?
This little devil is a *dolly*.

Hay un viejito que trabaja cargando bultos con un **diablito**.

There is an old man who works carrying large items with a *dolly*.

DIUREX

NEED some tape for a job at the office? Then ask for **diurex**, a brand name now applied to transparent tape, instead of the standard **cinta adhesiva**.

Rompí mis lentes y tuve que usarlos pegados con **diurex** por como dos meses.

I broke my glasses and had to use *Scotch tape* to hold them together for two months.

WILLINGNESS

¡A LO QUE TE TRUJE, CHENCHA!

LITERAL MEANING: TO WHAT I BROUGHT YOU HERE FOR, LITTLE CRESCENCIA!

LITTLE Crescencia, nicknamed Chencha, had just arrived at the house where she was to work as a maid. Shy and unsure where to begin, she just sat there. Perhaps that's when her new employer scolded her with the words above. Essentially, her boss was indicating that it was time to get to work. After all, that's why she was there. Pull out this saying when you've arrived on the scene, and your companions are in no hurry to get started. In my first month in the country, an associate invited me to a meeting. Once we arrived at the conference room, he asked if I could do a presentation. "Me? I just got here." I'll never forget his reply:

¡A lo que te truje, Chencha!

You're here to work, so work!

AVIADOR

LITERAL MEANING: AVIATOR

PILOTS don't stay long in one place. Their life is an endless series of takeoffs and landings. That's why an **aviador** comes and goes from work as he pleases; likely a relative hired him. Compare with #408, **aterrizar**.

Manuel trabaja en el gobierno, pero como **aviador**. Su tío es el director.

Manuel has a *cushy government job*. His uncle is the director.

CHACHAREAR

LITERAL MEANING: FRIVOLOUS CONVERSATION

LIKE to chew the fat? Shoot the breeze? That's the idea here. And when better to engage in idle talk than while shopping. For Mexicans, **chácharas** are *odds and ends*, or in good British English, *bits and bobs*. By extension the verb **chacharear** is the buying or selling of articles of little value. Yard sale, anyone?

> Voy a **chacharear** un rato.
>
> I'm going *walk around and see what they're selling* for a while.

DE OQUIS

DID you finish washing your car only to have it rain minutes later? Did you study many years in college only to discover you couldn't get a job in your field? If so, you can understand the phrase **de oquis**—*in vain*.

① Ser trabajadora es fácil, pero no me gusta estar en mi casa **de oquis**.
It's easy to be hard-working, but I don't like being home *doing nothing*.

② En mi rancho terminas de bañarte y sudas bien feo; eso me pone de malas porque sentí que me bañé **de oquis**.

Where I'm from you finish bathing and start sweating profusely. That puts me in a bad mood because I feel like I bathed *in vain*.

HACER ACTO DE PRESENCIA

LITERAL MEANING: TO MAKE AN ACT OF PRESENCE

DO you sometimes show up just because you have no other choice? Then you are merely present for appearances' sake.

> Solo **hago acto de presencia** en clases virtuales porque nunca pongo atención.
>
> I *merely show up* in virtual class, because I never pay attention.

HACER CONCHA

LITERAL MEANING: TO MAKE SHELL

TAKE out the trash! Make your bed! Go buy us some tortillas! What if those commands were directed to someone in a figurative shell? Would his muscles even twitch the slightest? Of course, not. The lazy person may become oblivious to the requests of those around him.

Le digo a mi hermano que me ayude a limpiar, pero solo **hace concha**.

I tell my brother to help me clean, but *he's lazy and couldn't care less.*

The Golden Pilón

5 01 *The Golden Pilón*

LO BAILADO NADIE ME LO QUITA.
LITERAL MEANING: WHAT I HAVE DANCED, NO ONE CAN TAKE AWAY FROM ME.

CONGRATULATIONS! Having completed this linguistic mouth-burning, you are now the proud possessor of more than 500 of the most colorful words, idioms and sayings that make Mexican Spanish *Mexican*. May these fiery words forever burn in your memory as you call on them time and again. As a collection they constitute the tongue that burned my mouth.

We conclude with this saying from a culture that loves to dance: **Lo bailado nadie me lo quita**. What have you experienced so far in life? How many jobs have you had? Which places have you visited? Which languages have you learned? Whatever the case, this adage reminds us that our life experience is unique. Your singular memories are yours only; your journey—whatever it may be—is one-of-a-kind. And that is something that no one can ever take from you.

Forgot what a **pilón** is? Go back to #361, **pilón**.

Acknowledgements

A WORK of this sort can never be accomplished without the help of many contributors.

Foremost of all, I thank my wife Moraima for her continued suggestions and encouragement. Since she is a **chicana** (see term #317), she has unwittingly been teaching me this dialect for almost thirty years now. Some of the terms in this volume I originally heard from her lips.

Thanks as well to Jason and Emily Provchy for the office space provided me during the preparation of this volume. Much gratitude goes also to Debbie Saucedo for her insightful observations on the naturalness of expressions both in English as well as Spanish. Esteban Hernández likewise provided key suggestions to enhance the authenticity of the expressions chosen. I still fondly remember Esteban for being the first person to use saying #76 **Si te digo que la burra es parda, es porque traigo los pelos en la mano** in a real-life setting. Yuri Malacara, who hails from the southern part of the country, cleared up details about some of Mexico's most beautiful traditional sayings together with their origins. Jason Provchy, Julie Pfouts, and Raquel Borrego provided timely insight into the English translations of the selected terms and contributed in making them more natural and accurate.

Lastly, I am indebted to the people of Mexico, for their painstaking patience with all of us foreigners who have learned your most colorful iteration of Spanish one explanation at a time.

Index

A

Photo Credits

Cover Flame • pixabay.com/darkmoon_art | Hot pepper cartoon • pixabay.com/Ega Maulana | Big tongue • Illustration 24388179 © Brett Lamb • Dreamstime.com | Volkswagen Bus Vector • freevector.com | textured paper • unsplash.com/Kiwihug | Turkey vector • studiogstock • freepik.com | Comic face expressions set • pch.vector • freepik.com| Mexican woman with sombrero • unsplash.com/Miguel González | Smiling with my yellow necktie • freeimages.com/Mario Alberto Magallanes Trejo | Mexican 20-cent coin • Lee Jamison| red pepper • mates • fotolia.com | **Running Headers** chili pepper • chili pepper by Thays Malcher from the Noun Project| Big tongue • Illustration 24388179 © Brett Lamb • Dreamstime.com | **Chapter Head** corn tortilla on white background • ID 150330851 © Chernetskaya • Dreamstime.com | **Chapter 1** Vector cactus hand-drawn poster • Illustration 76851461 © Alenakarabanova • Dreamstime.com | **2** Homenaje a Cantinflas • Daniel Alvarado Silvera, Wikipedia Commons | **11** Population of Our World • iStock.com/tom-iurchenko | **15** birds on wire • freeimages.com/Ondrej Verzich | **23** Smiling with my yellow necktie • freeimages.com/Mario Alberto Magallanes Trejo | **30** umbrella 3 • freeimages.com/ Elvis Santana | **38** dog wagging tail • pixabay.com/Clker-Free-Vector-Images| **50** Mexican 20-cent coin • Lee Jamison | **54** beating heart • pixabay.com/OpenClipart-Vectors | **64** Couple Choosing Wide TV With Shop Assistant Help • ID 86305419 © Evgenii Naumov • Dreamstime.com | **66** time running • pixabay.com/Gerd Altmann | **Chapter 2** Mexican Chihuahua • © Adobe Stock, Javier brosch | **76 Box** Crazy Chicken • Illustration 29371938 © Ratoca • Dreamstime.com | **83** ant • unsplash.com/Peter F. Wolf | **90** A cartoon dog scratches the fleas off of his body • Illustration 40497867 © Brett Lamb • Dreamstime.com | **99** Colorful Rooster Sleeping on Pillow, Farm Cock Cartoon Character Vector Illustration • © Adobe Stock, topvectors | **106** Cute funny crying worm with tears isolated on white background • © Adobe Stock, zionbalkon | **111** A cartoon mouse reading a big book • ID 9001740 © Sarah Holmlund • Dreamstime.com | **Chapter 3** human anatomy drawing, old, canvas • © Adobe Stock, adimas | **120** chucks • pixabay.com/Open-Clipart-Vectors | **126** hanger • pixabay.com/ChaminaGallery | **130** blue jeans isolated on white • ID 126824335 © Aurinko • Dreamstime.com | **136** Huaraches Guandarría by Huaraches Jamay • By Huaracheblog - Own work, CC Commons| **140** Hair clipper isolated on white • © Adobe Stock, Nikcoa | **144** Painful bump • ID 41570470 © Brett Lamb • Dreamstime.com | **152** A laughing cartoon man with a huge mouth with only a few teeth • © Adobe Stock, blambca | **159** Photo of beautiful housekeeper with credit card in hand • Designed by drobotean/ Freepic.com | **Chapter 4** Mexican woman in native garb • pixabay.com/Rebeca Cruz Galván | **162** Thumbs up • © Adobe Stock, Sergey Nivens | **172** girl and boy talking • pixabay.com/Mote Oo Education | **175** husband wife hugging • pixabay.com/Clker-Free-Vector-Images | **Chapter 5** candle in hands • pixabay.com/Myriam Zilles | **187** Rat • ID 27948379 © Amplion • Dreamstime.com | **190** Jarabe Mexico National Dance Mexican Hat Dance • ID 59024615 © Brancaescova • Dreamstime.com | **200** Big and funny clowns photos • Photo 34065038 © Ababaka | Dreamstime.com | **205** A vector illustration of a bronco rider in a rodeo ID 133401311 © Fredweiss • Dreamstime.com | **213** angry and

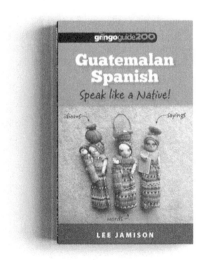